BECOMING
WHO GOD
INTENDED

BECOMING WHO GOD INTENDED

DAVID ECKMAN

BECOMING WHO GOD INTENDED

To the greatest of supporters—

Carol Eckman
Adrianne Eckman
Andrew Eckman

Acknowledgments

Hundreds of people could be acknowledged in the making of this book. Many of them are brothers and sisters in Christ who have opened their hearts and shared their pilgrimages and experiences under the grace of God the Father. These of the transparent heart (an uncommon virtue), I thank.

A personal thanks has to go to the board leadership of Becoming What God Intended Seminars: Bob Ladd, chairman (an older brother and father in the Lord), and Steve Noble (a man whose name truly befits him). All of the board members are an affinity group of the best sort.

To my co-founder, Bill Lauer—I feel deep appreciation for this man of a servant's heart (which is code for, "He does what I really don't want to do"). Other team members have sustained me with their love and affection.

Sheri and Kevin Osborn are to be thanked for their generous gifts to the seminar ministry specifically to release time for me to work on this book. Such thanks also go to the directors of the Howard and Betty White Foundation.

The publishers of Harvest House have been examples of what people in such a crucial position should be. To my fellow pilgrim Paul Gossard, the editor, I have nothing but affection and admiration. He has made this project a joy. His insight into the significance and his understanding of what is on these pages is a rare gift to me.

To my wife, Carol, and our grown children, Adrianne and Andrew, to whom this book is dedicated—we fly on each other's affection and support!

Contents

Why Hasn't
the Truth Touched
Our Hearts?

You haven't worked hard enough.

You aren't praying or reading the Bible enough.

The difficulty you're experiencing is a punishment because your Christian life isn't good enough.

Kim, who had come up to speak to me during a break in a seminar, was using these phrases to describe how her mind would worry, work, and try to figure out how she could please God—how she could earn His love and acceptance.

Our team had just finished sharing about how people's family backgrounds influence how they function in relationships as adults. We had emphasized how a Christian's relationship to God is often defined through the mental pictures that come out of those backgrounds. Kim, along with her friend Charlene, had been in a Bible study together using some of our material. Now these two women, as well as their husbands, had come up to the front of the auditorium. Their happy and excited expressions made a strong contrast to the story Kim was telling.

She had grown up in the church and had a more than well-trained conscience to prove it. She had continually been beaten up by it and, as a result, discouragement and depression had been her constant companions. "And I was so tired," she continued. "I didn't feel worthy of love, and I was afraid to try to love others." Her view of God and the pictures she carried around in her heart had damaged her emotions, and those damaged emotions had been tormenting her.

Then, in the study she and Charlene were in, she had come across a biblical word picture that had changed all that.

Her new perspective on the truth had a great impact. "Probably the most gratifying of all is the joy of the freedom that energizes me to want to obey God and love my neighbor," she said. "I love to share these truths and wonderful word pictures with fellow Christians who struggle."

When I am talking to a couple, I always carefully watch (hopefully without being noticed) the partner who is listening. A spouse's positive reaction is always a powerful proof of a deep change in the life. In this case, Kim's husband was smiling more broadly than she was.

The Christianity that had promised to meet the greatest needs of their hearts had finally worked.

Charlene then spoke up. While Kim's challenge was related to what her church background had taught her, Charlene's pain had come from a heartbreaking family background, in particular her relationship with her mother. "My mom would beat me…and what really killed me inside was that my dad wouldn't stop her," she said.

The pictures we carry around in our hearts have a direct impact on our emotions. In Charlene's case, the pictures were not religious, as were Kim's, but were memories of a dark and sad past. She, like Kim, had found relief and freedom through the study they were doing together.

Both of these women had their deep needs met. The Christianity that had promised to meet the greatest needs of their hearts had *finally* worked. It was not that Christianity had changed—rather, their understanding of Christianity had changed in a rich and profound way.

How many times I've heard stories like this from Christians who have attended church for years—Bible-teaching churches with competent pastors who are known for giving solid sermons from the Scriptures!

Why is it that the truth—good, solid, biblical truth—that believers have heard hundreds of times has not changed them? How can we as believers experience this truth in a way that's effective? As we explore these questions, may you also discover how Christianity can meet the deepest needs of your heart!

PART 1

Did God Make a Mistake When He Gave Us Emotions?

1

Sure, I'm a Christian, But—

🌿 🌿 🌿

YOU MAY NOT HAVE A LIFE STORY like that of Kim or Charlene. But inside, your heart may be just as hurt or empty. Week after week you go to church, knowing you're going to heaven and believing that the Bible is full of good truths to live by.

In your heart of hearts, though—where you really live, feel, and think—God seems irrelevant. The Bible doesn't seem to apply. You feel disconnected from others and from God Himself.

Having feelings that do not match our expectation of what the Christian life should be is common. Perhaps your experience matches that of one very sincere man I got to know:

> I struggled with the inability to connect my emotions to my beliefs. For example, when I committed a sin, I would ask for forgiveness, but not "feel" forgiven. I would continue to ask and ask, even though I "knew" that God answered prayers. So why didn't I feel forgiven?
>
> Then there was my "personal" relationship with Christ. This issue had caused me some discomfort over the years. My understanding of Christ and His death on the cross was

something like this: Jesus died for all of humanity. In the pile called humanity, if you looked hard, you would find me. I just got included with the masses. This was a pretty non-personal relationship, but it was the best I could muster.

This next man's struggle did not revolve around not having emotions, but having too many of the wrong kind.

The picture I had created was one of a heavenly Father that kept a scorecard of my every move, with very little patience for my continual sin and often holding back His love and blessings because of that. Go talk to prisoners on Sunday after church—up three points. Swear at the guy who is tailgating me down the hill afterward—down two points. The "performance" thinking was at work in my life without my realizing it or being able to relieve the guilt I often felt. I was always asking God the same question: *Am I still worthy?*

The natural result of these experiences is that what is going on in the inside is at odds with what's on the outside. And many believers end up feeling as though the following describes the "normal Christian life":

I believed that God was a judging God who constantly condemned me for my actions. My solution was to work hard to earn His favor by dedicating my life to ministry and reading the Bible. I was involved full-time in various ministries. I spent a couple of hours a day praying and studying God's Word. My actions looked good on the outside, but my inside emotions and thoughts did not go along with my actions. The people around me thought that I was a good Christian because they did not know what was going on inside of me.

A Disconnected Life

There is a wide and gaping hole in the lives of many believers. Most Christians are aware that God is a God of unconditional love, unbelievable acceptance, and inexhaustible compassion. They would even say they believe these things. But very few of them are living a joyful Christian life because *their emotions are not connected to the truth about who God is.* The inability to connect emotions to the truth is one of the most tragic circumstances facing the church today.

Let us see how this comes about. First, Christians believe that Christ died for all of their sins, but often they unconsciously disconnect particular sins and certain acts they are ashamed of from the benefits of that truth. Why do they do that? None of us likes to dwell even a second on stuff that makes us feel like worthless wretches. We take a child's approach to those things. If it feels bad, we avoid it. As we do this avoiding, we miss the opportunity to really get the truth of God's love and forgiveness worked into our heart.

Second, we simply do not slow down (or someone else does not slow us down) so we can connect the dots. We jump on the superhighway of church life, and the next thing we know we are on three committees—out each night of the week—and losing our temper over every little thing. So that Christian truth is really connected to our inner life, we need to slow down and take a slow tour of Christianity—and a slow walk around the cross. (You'll see what I mean by that later in this chapter.)

But what is the most effective way of doing that? What I hear over again and again is that the Bible teaching people hear in the seminars we give is not new. But for some reason, it has a profoundly different effect this time. The truths are brought home with great power, and the hearers finally connect them with their emotions!

Why? *Personalized pictures of truth.* Pictures are a large part of the answer. The truths of our acceptance in the love relationship of the Father, Son, and Holy Spirit, our redemption, and our identification with Christ are presented as pictures the listeners participate in.

A Picture Changed My Life

If we don't see life from God's perspective and learn to participate in His pictures of the truth, at best our emotions may remain frozen, or at worse be immensely negative. In my own life, God's pictures did two very powerful things: they made the truth personal to me, and they deeply touched my emotions.

I stumbled onto this principle years ago as I was reading the Bible one day. At the time my emotional life was frozen. The reason for that was my family background. I grew up in a non-Christian home with an alcoholic dad who tore down everyone around him. This led me to shut off my emotions. Throughout the two decades of my growing-up years, Dad would start drinking on Friday night and become stranger and stranger as the weekend went on. To deal with the discomfort and pain caused by his endless bitterness about life, I turned my emotions off more and more. By the time I became an adult, I hardly felt anything. As a cover I perfected appearing amiable and cheerful, but nothing was underneath—just a void.

I became a Christian at 17 and a pastor at 25. Conversion and an immense amount of Bible information did not melt the ice cube within. Of course I dutifully read the Bible and prayed. But nothing changed. At the same time one of the crazy beliefs that

Christians somehow pick up was tormenting me. The belief was that God cared about people only *after* they became Christians.

With that came a heartbreaking suspicion I didn't dare express to anyone: *Didn't God care about what my family and I had suffered? Did it matter to Him at all what my brothers and mother and I had gone through with a drunken dad? Did God not have any pity and concern for us then?*

The question was so troubling I was afraid to ask anyone. I was afraid to pray about it. To show how unwilling a person can be to ask fearful questions, I did not try to get the question answered in college or in seminary...nor did I face it in my first years of pastoring. I was studying the Bible all the time, but I was not connecting what it said with my question.

In fact, I had very little emotional connection of any kind to the truth of the gospel and the Bible. I became a Christian fanatic about those things, but I did not *feel* them. I became a pastor who practiced appearing friendly but who felt very little inside. What else would you expect from someone who was not certain God had compassion on his family's suffering?

In my 30s the question was still not asked, and it continued to gnaw away. The picture I had in my imagination was that of an uncaring dad...so why should I not instinctively assume that God, the "Ultimate Dad," wouldn't care about the pain of my family? Wasn't He a dad? I was used to dads not caring.

The Change

One day I was casually reading the Bible. When I reached the words of Ephesians 2:4—"God, continually being rich in mercy, because of His great passionate delight with which He passionately loved us"—my mind was suddenly plunged into a picture.

I was six. I was back in our home again. Looming over me as I was cowering in a chair was my dad in his 40s. Drunk, he was telling me over and over what a disappointment I was to him, going on and on. To my left, in the corner of the room, there was a window with a table and a lamp in front of it. The window was broken—it had happened a day or two before. (Alcoholics are slow to fix things.)

I glanced out through the six-inch hole in the glass…and I saw the face of God. Tears were rolling down His cheeks.

All of this took place in my imagination. It wasn't a vision…at least I don't think it was. But instantly, I knew exactly what it meant. It meant that God had cared. He had been concerned— He had cried over how we had lived as non-Christians. He may not have been the God of our home back then, but He had access—the window was broken, and He could get in. At the point of my greatest humiliation, *He cared.*

Suddenly a deep change occurred within. I felt the compassion of God enter my heart. With it came an eruption of emotions, an almost physical sensation of an ice cube within melting into warmth. I began to feel again! Those emotions, and the sense of the compassion of God, have stayed with me since that day.

That picture in my heart was a turning point in my life. And over time, I became more and more aware of what a powerful hold, for bad or good, the pictures in our imagination have on us.

The Picture You Have to Start From

Sometimes God's greatest truths are hidden by the words we use about them. We don't understand them because we don't relate them to our own life experience—as was the case with me—or those who are teaching forget to instruct us to picture ourselves in those truths. And when we do not picture ourselves in the truths of the Bible, we do not experience those truths in our heart.

Before we look at a key example of a biblical picture, take a look at the following diagram. It will help you get an idea of how the pictures in our imagination affect everything "down the line." As we talk more about the elements shown in the diagram, especially our emotions, we'll continue to refer to it.

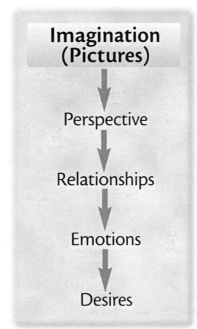

The greatest example of a biblical picture we are completely immersed in is the cross. Understanding what God did at the cross is the basis for our growth in the Christian life. But for the cross to become real to us, we must *experience it in our emotions.* We're going to talk about biblical pictures in much more detail in Part 2, but let's get a taste of what God intends us to use the imagination for. Take a few minutes to turn loose that wonderful ability that God has given you. The imagination can be used for wretched pictures or great pictures, and too often we use it the wrong way. Let's use it the right way!

Imagine a Walk with God to the Cross

Take a moment to imagine the time in your life when you committed your most embarrassing sin or set of sins. (Or sometimes it's not a particular sin or shameful pattern but a particular event that emotionally blackmails Christians—a divorce, for example.) Whatever it is, picture that time. Dredge it up. Pull it up into your awareness, no matter how red-faced you get. The sin might have been only a trifle, or it might have been something terrible. I am not asking you to dwell on it—just bring it up long enough so that you feel the discomfort of the emotions.

Once you have it in your mind, imagine that in the midst of committing that sin or suffering that event, you hear a knocking at the door. The knocking is steady and persistent. You know you must answer it. In great embarrassment and discomfort you go to the door. Your mind races, wondering who it might be... *The neighbors? The police? Your spouse?* Whoever it is, you know you have been found out at your most shameful, guilty, painful moment.

You open the door in great fear—but to your surprise, you are met with the most understanding and compassionate expression you have ever seen in your life. The individual at the door looks in your eyes and says, "I am God the Father. I have picked out this moment because I need to talk with you. Let's go for a walk."

You do not refuse. With great hesitation, you step out beside Him. His knock, His voice, His face all communicate massive power and authority. Now He looks at you again with that same striking expression—total understanding marked by real compassion. He says, "I know you are weak. I know what you were doing. I know, whether you recognize it or not, that you intensely dislike Me. And I know that deep at the core you're ungodly—you have no great interest in a relationship with Me. *But I need to share with you that We are the only ones who know who you are.* You *don't even know who you are.* You are chained by guilt, bound by shame, and filled with deep resentment. You are in a fog of guilt, shame, and bad memories—but *We* see through the fog.

"But I can see beyond your problems, and I can see someone you have never seen—I can see *you.* Because I know who you are, I've intervened at this moment to show you what you are worth to my Son and Me."

> *"My Son is dying for you because you are worth a Son to Me."*

Since you went out through the door, you've been hanging your head, staring at your feet. Too overwhelmed by your own feelings, you do not realize the Father has been walking you up a slight slope. Your heart is ricocheting between the embarrassment of true red-handed guilt…and awe at the presence of such a powerful and compassionate Person.

In a kind way He touches your shoulder with His hand and turns you to face the east. He directs your eyes to a hillside, where you see a young man on a cross. His face radiates that same astonishing expression—total understanding marked by real compassion. You suddenly realize the Man on the cross is His Son. The Father says quietly, "We picked this strategic moment: this moment of great weakness. We didn't pick the moment in the future when you would be healthy. We chose this moment to show you how serious We are about this and how significant you are to Us. My Son is dying for you because *you are worth a Son to Me.* You are worth more than your guilt. We are the only ones who know who you are! We know who you are, and I love you."

The Starting Point for Healthy Emotions

This picture is deeply biblical, for everything that God wants to communicate to us begins at the cross. All positive and profound changes in our emotions must begin as our imagination is penetrated with this truth: When we had the least to offer, He offered the Son. Romans 5:5-6 teaches us that God wants us to connect our great weakness and shame to His Son's great work on the Cross:

> Hope does not put us to shame, because God's passionate delight has been poured out into our hearts through the Holy Spirit that has been given to us. For Christ, while we were still morally helpless, yet died at the right season for the ungodly.*

God wants us to view the cross in a certain way—as an expression of His love and affection for us. Romans 5:8 says that "God recommends, or demonstrates, His agape love for us in that while we were continually sinners Christ died for us."

God does not love us for what we will become or what He is going to turn us into. This is the whole point of the passage. God allowed His only Son, Jesus Christ, to die for us at the moment that was most strategic to establish our worth to Him—our worst moment—so we could recognize the incredible fact that His interest in us is based *only on who we are to Him.*

---

* Unless otherwise noted, the Bible translations used throughout the book are my own. They are true to the Greek and Hebrew texts. My desire is to give a rich and expanded but accurate translation of what God has to say through His Word.

God recommends His agape love to us because He wants us to share in it. As we will see more of later, God's love is a passionate delight in His own. It is not just a teeth-gritting act of His will, but an ocean of passionate liking! He honestly thinks that the best thing we can do for ourselves is to know His love.

This may not be what we are used to, but our obligation is simply to understand it enough so that we start dancing and jumping up and down like little kids. Children melt down into glee when they meet a relative who likes them. That's the response we are supposed to have. Christians need to walk to the cross every day of their lives to ignite the torch of God's love in their hearts.

🍃 🍃 🍃

It's Time to Change the Pictures

Pictures penetrate where thoughts cannot. They change the heart's emotions when teaching cannot. Pictures seem to be God's way of opening up our hearts when they are hurt and alienated.

Since the day God dropped the picture of His love for me and my family into my mind, by slow crawl and sometimes by accident—and more deliberately over the passage of time—I have added word-picture stories to my Bible teaching. Always I place my listeners in the scene and the action. These stories have become a potent tool to make the truth personal to struggling Christians, and over the years tens of thousands of people have seen their lives transformed in this way by the truth of the Bible.

God did not just send us a dictionary—He sent us a text that contains vivid pictures. He did not just send us a book—He sent Christ as a living illustration of His love. Heaven gave us one central picture of the Father's love: the cross. As we saw in the word picture, we need to walk to the cross in our weakest moments, our greatest sins, and our deepest shames. This is where we need to begin in grasping the depth of our relationship with Him and the depth of His love for us.

In our hearts, each of us carries around pictures, both good and bad, that have been passed on to us...almost like a family picture album. Just as I had a picture of God as an uncaring dad, all of us have been emotionally affected by the pictures that come from our family background, whether that family was healthy, confused, or severely stressed. In the coming pages we will see how each of these family backgrounds produces a different set of pictures.

Now is the time to change the set. Let's collect a new, good set from the Bible about our new family—the family of God.

The rest of this book contains more powerful truths about our acceptance by the Father, Son, and Holy Spirit, and about our identity in Christ—and these truths are presented in the form of life-changing pictures. As you read further, let the truth and the pictures change you!

2

Trapped in
the Mood Cycle

PING. PING. A few minutes passed, and there it was again. *Ping.* The sound was coming from the backyard. It was early evening and it was dark outside. At the time my wife, Carol, and I were living in a two-story Victorian home right outside of San Francisco. I opened up the upstairs back window and looked out into the night. In the yard next door, I saw our neighbor Rob shining a flashlight. Rob was a friendly, gregarious guy, so I asked him about the noise I'd heard. "Oh," he said, "I'm shooting snails."

"You're doing *what?*"

"I'm shooting snails with my BB gun," he replied. Sure enough, in one hand he held a flashlight and in the other, a BB gun. In California, where we live, snails are everywhere, and anyone who wants to grow anything has to deal with them. Normally we use bait. Shooting them with BBs seemed unique.

"Hey, this is fun," Rob shouted to me, "and a great way to relax. Come on over and shoot a few." I said no thanks, and then joked that the reason he was using the flashlight was to spotlight the snails like deer, blinding them so they wouldn't move and he could shoot them. I thought my comment was hilarious, but Rob didn't laugh.

Though perhaps my humor fell short, I actually think Rob didn't laugh because his snail hunting was a serious attempt to deal with anxiety. He was a law student who was getting ready for the bar exam. He was very, very nervous about it because the majority of people who took it failed. He had been doing a whole bunch of things to keep his anxiety under control, and snail hunting was the latest and most bizarre thing so far.

People do a lot of things to deal with anxiety, and snail hunting is probably one of the less harmful ways of dealing with it (unless you are a snail). If we could all go snail hunting to control our emotions it could be a great deal of fun, but probably for most people it will not do the trick. Emotions are important to understand and manage, and when they are not managed, they can be dangerous.

The Crucial Place of Emotions

It is not the negative emotion itself—such as my neighbor's anxiety—that is the only problem. As we go through this chapter, we'll see that anxiety and other negative emotions set up what I call the *mood cycle*. This cycle is one of the major unaddressed realities in the life of many people, and it is a major issue in the Bible. And if we catch an understanding of what it is, then we'll see how we can deal with character issues, addictions, and sins in our lives in a much different and positive way. We can use the personalized pictures of the truth I described in chapter 1 to powerfully address this cycle.

There is another reason why emotions are so important: They're more than just what we *feel*. They are a major part of *being human*—as much of who we are as thinking, imagining, willing, and relating. They create the atmosphere for life—our internal weather, so to speak. Not only do we have the spiritual responsibility of dealing with our lusts, or desires to sin (as well as having the responsibility not to sin), but we also have the responsibility of changing the "weather" within.

The wonderful truth is, we can effectively change the weather inside us by using the pictures and relationships the Bible provides. If we change that weather, we disperse the storm clouds that bring on the rest of the mood cycle. Managing moods leads to a managed and happy life.

Unmanaged moods (negative emotions) do more than just hurt inside—they lead people down a path to sin. They lead people down the path of the works of the flesh and into addiction. They lead people to death. Christians often naively assume that morality is just a matter of just saying no—just a matter of black-and-white choices. But before the choice, before the question of right and wrong, before we do the evil act or noble deed, we have to do something with our emotions. And what we do with our emotions will almost predetermine what we do with our will and relationships. This reality is explained in the mood cycle.

Understanding the Mood Cycle

First, though, we need to know how that cycle works. It starts with a negative and powerful mood that produces or is captivated by a strong desire, which, when acted on, results in sin. Much too often we notice the sin—the result—but do not notice the process or the underlying mood. Noticing the mood is critically important.

One Saturday I was working out in the garage while my wife, Carol, was working in the house. On days we're doing this, as often as not she will come to the door of the garage and say, "Isn't this fun?" (Her idea of a great date is working around the house. That is not my picture of flaming romance, however.)

Unfortunately, I am not a garage person or a project person. Usually I do this kind of work because I love Carol and want to do things that make her happy. Since most of the time I am simply working out there for her sake, I am impatient and want the job over with.

On this particular Saturday, I hit my hand with a hammer. Already tired and frustrated, now I was annoyed with myself and in pain. When Carol came to the garage door and asked for my help on another project, I blew up. "Can't you see I'm busy?" I demanded angrily. (For us angry words are rare, so she was surprised and so was I. Shortly afterward I went in and apologized.)

But notice that the undercurrent really set me up for the outburst. If I had been rested and not frustrated, and had not hit my hand, my poor wife would not have become the target of my angry response. The emotions inside of me were the mood. The mood is the negative and powerful emotions floating around on the inside. Then, something or someone draws a desire from us on the outside. What comes out, comes out powerfully! My desire was to be left alone in my misery, my wife provoked that desire, and I exploded with anger.

The Elements of the Cycle

Many people do not realize that an unhappy heart is easy to tempt. Or to put it in other more positive terms, happy people are hard to tempt. The first element in the mood cycle, unhappiness of some sort, is not there. But temptation is powerfully heightened when the heart is hurting and unhappy. That's the first part of the mood cycle. Then, a desire arises that pulls the person away and the last step is wrongdoing or sin. The order of the cycle is *mood, desire,* and then *sin.*

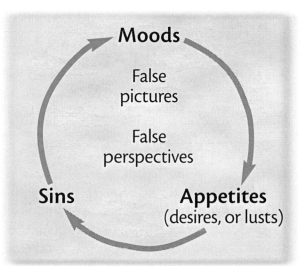

Paul the apostle isolated the elements of the mood cycle. In Galatians 5:24 he wrote, "Those who belong to Christ Jesus have crucified the flesh as a way of life with its passions, or moods, and desires." Many believers will notice that desires or lusts are associated with the flesh, but they may overlook the other term, the English word "passions." The flesh has two powerful weapons it uses. One is lust, or desire, and the other is *passion*.

Passion is more than romance. That romantic meaning is what most people are aware of, but in life and the Bible it is used for far more. Somebody might say to me, "What is your passion?"—in other words, "What are the powerful emotions that are driving your life?" That is the way Paul is using the term—except for him these are the passions, or moods, of the flesh, so they are not good passions. This is key to understanding the mood cycle:

> 🦋 *Passions* refer to those strong emotions that create a negative, uncomfortable atmosphere, even a painful atmosphere, within. *Desires,* or *lusts,* come out of those moods (passions) and lead us outwardly to do something wrong.

❦ *Lusts* lead us outwardly, after we have become inwardly enveloped with moods.

Let me explain how this works again, using an old movie as an illustration. I was little when I first saw *The Creature from the Black Lagoon*. It was unforgettably scary to a boy of six. As the story line went, a monster lived in a swamp—and if you were canoeing in that swamp, the "creature" would come out of the water and get you. For our purposes, the swamp is the moods, and the "creature" is the lusts that come out of that swamp and overpower us. Drain the swamp and the creature is finished! Drain the moods, and the lusts (desires, or appetites) of the flesh are weak and easy to push aside.

Why We Can't Ignore the Mood Cycle

If we look at the New Testament carefully, we will see that it has two types of commands: commands that address our appetites (our lusts), and commands that address our moods (our passions). Take a look for instance, at Christ's command in Matthew 6:25:

> On account of this I am telling you, stop worrying about your life, what you will be eating or drinking; or about your body, what you will be wearing. Is not life more important than food, and the body more important than clothes?

Christ considers our moods, such as anxiety and worry, important enough that He addressed them at length in the Sermon on the Mount. What is absolutely fascinating is that Christ's answer to some anxieties and other moods is to change the pictures within the heart. (We will look at that carefully in chapter 5.)

Sexual Sin and the Cycle

Indeed addressing moods is a strategic part of the spiritual life. For a major example, our Christian culture overemphasizes dealing with lust but often overlooks the "turbocharger" of passions. For many Christians that is where the real battle is.

As a pastor for 16 years, and as a Bible teacher and counselor for many additional years, I have been asked numerous times to deal with persons who find themselves in adulterous relationships. Usually when I talk to the person who has broken their marriage vow, he or she will inform me that the affair is the greatest relationship ever experienced. Surprisingly people in affairs will say that they have never been more alive.

Telling them, though, that what they are doing is wrong is just not a new revelation. They know that very well. Often I take a different approach. I don't talk to them about what's going on outside—the affair—but I talk to them about what is going on inside. I start talking to them about the emotions in their life, and eventually I tell them about the mood cycle.

For the troubled married couple, the mood cycle starts with an undercurrent of strong negative emotion that often goes unnoticed. For example, the emotion might be loneliness. The marriage has become two people living under the same roof who hardly talk to each other. Neither realized the loneliness they were feeling was an important symptom of a marriage in the doldrums, suffering from neglect. Instead the couple busied themselves with work and hobbies. Romance was neglected; conversations became more and more infrequent; boredom with the relationship was tolerated. Or perhaps a lack of forgiveness created bitterness and indifference.

A friend of mine was discovered in an affair, and all the elements were there. As their children entered their teenage years, the couple had slowly grown apart. She poured herself into the children; he poured himself into ministry. Neither of them paid all that much attention to how lonely they felt. Nor did they work on nurturing their own relationship. He seemed to deal with the pain in his own life by working harder and harder. Finally the vulnerable minister met a vulnerable woman, and the two became involved. As he tried to extricate himself, he told me he had never felt so alive as he had while experiencing the affair. Sadly, that may well have been the case—because his inner life had died years before. He just had not noticed it. When he got himself into the excitement of an illicit relationship, the pleasure masked the undercurrent of pain and supplied some enjoyment.

Negative emotions unaddressed are relationally and spiritually dangerous.

Sometimes (unfortunately, not all the time does it work) when I begin to ask the person caught up in an affair about the underlying emotional current in the marriage and within their heart, a profound change takes place. Instead of telling me about this new relationship and the adventure of it, the person begins to speak of disappointed dreams in marriage, hurts in life, goals never attained, and sadness that really has never gone away. As we explore those underlying moods, I begin to share how those painful emotions can be left behind and the marriage can ultimately be restored. As the conversation deepens, and especially if the person is open to talk about what is going on inside, the affair may be left behind. To really have a change, the person needs not only to call sin, sin, but also needs to learn how to change the emotions within. For if those emotions do not change, then the repentance is just mental, and the person is still vulnerable. Negative emotions unaddressed are relationally and spiritually dangerous.

The Basic Emotions of the Christian Life

As we have seen, Paul the apostle gave desires and moods as the two great weapons of the flesh. He said that in a context that describes how the spiritual life works—Galatians 5, where he wrote about a life influenced by the Spirit of God. Before he mentioned the twin weapons of the flesh, passions (moods) and strong desire, he mentioned the works of the flesh. Note the list.

> Now the habits or works of the flesh are evident, which are: sexual immorality, dirty-mindedness, and indecency, idolatry, sorcery, hatred, strife, jealousy, outbursts of anger, disputes, dissensions, factions, envying, drunkenness, carousing, and things like these, of which I told you before just as I have forewarned you that those who are practicing such things shall not inherit the kingdom of God (verses 19-21).

Notice the various addictive and dangerous behaviors that are present: sexual addiction with sexual immorality and carousing; rageaholism with enmity; strife; outbursts of anger, disputes, and dissensions; and alcoholism with drunkenness. But scattered among those terms are negative moods, like impurity and sensuality, jealousy, and envy. Those inner emotions are as important or even more important than the desires.

Here again we have the three elements of the mood cycle: passion (moods), desire (lust), and sin (the works of the flesh). Without the mood the desire would not be empowered. Without the empowered desire you would not have the work of the flesh, the addictive behavior that is sin.

Then Paul described the opposite of those moods when he gave the fruit of the Spirit, which starts with love, joy, and peace.

> But the fruit of the Spirit is passionate delight in people, deep satisfaction with life, peace, patience, kindness, goodness, faithfulness, meekness, self-control; against such there is no law (verse 22).

One simple definition of a passion, or a mood, is whatever inward emotional state is the opposite to the fruit of the Spirit. A peaceful, loving, happy heart can easily brush aside temptation. Anything that is opposite to those three—love, joy, and peace—then may well qualify as a mood or passion. It's a crucial thing to understand, however, that these positive emotions are to be the foundational emotions of a Christian's heart. (We'll spend more time developing this truth in chapter 4.)

The Addictive Pattern

When a person is inundated with moods that are out of control and appetites that are endangering health, relationships, and life, the root cause is unaddressed emotions. We have looked a little bit at the mood cycle, but there is also what is called the addictive pattern. Both start at the same point, unaddressed emotional (and for addiction sometimes physical) pain. Mismanaging painful emotions within plunges millions into a slavery that may eventually take their lives. Knowing how to manage emotions is actually *lifesaving*. The great news is that the Christian spiritual life is especially designed to deal with emotional pain.

Pain and Addiction

A lot of research has gone into how addiction works, and one of the more popular theories—which I subscribe to—is that addiction starts when inner pain is incorrectly addressed. The person in pain merely reacts to it instead of investigating why it is there and meaningfully addressing the stress.

Addiction, in its essence, is using something enjoyable to kill pain in the life and bring some pleasure. That is how the mood cycle works also, but many times the negative effects are not as obvious in the mood cycle as they are in addiction.

Many people naively assume that all it takes to deal with addictions (alcoholism, drugs, misuse of prescription drugs, sex addiction, and others) is will power. Will power alone will not work. What makes lusts and desires so addictive is the pain that is beneath. It is like the vast build-up under a volcano that finally explodes with incredible force when it finds an outlet to the surface.

For a number of years I would teach once a month at what was called a "Higher Power" Service. That was a Friday-night meeting that compulsive and addicted people would attend to learn about addiction and how Christ could help them. Several hundred of the most hard-looking people I have ever seen in my life would show up. (At the end, the managers of the meeting would sign attendance forms for the parole officers of many who were there.)

The group would have music, testimonials, and a teaching time. As I would teach I would ask questions. (It was about as good a "focus group" as you could ever get on addiction.) One time I asked, "Is it the addiction—sex, drugs, alcohol, whatever it is—or is it the pain in your lives that is the great enemy of your recovery?" I asked for a show of hands. "How many believe it is the pain, as opposed to the addiction, that is the real enemy?" Every person in the room either said yes or nodded their head or raised their hand, affirming they fully understood it was emotional pain that was driving the addiction.

I was often asked back to speak at these recovery meetings because I would talk about how the negative pictures in our hearts added to the pain or created the pain that we carry. I would teach the listeners about the new pictures that they needed. I told them they had far more ability to control and manage their emotions than they had ever thought. But they had to change the pictures in their hearts.

Robots in Pain

What happens with addiction is that when discomfort enters the soul, the person develops robotlike habits to deal with the pain and gain some pleasure. Binge eaters frequently do this. They feel some discomfort then robotically pursue a pleasure to deal with discomfort.

Several years ago my daughter, Adrianne, asked me to go with her to Weight Watchers. She first asked Carol if she could go with her, but it could not be fit into Carol's schedule. Adrianne then asked me. She was 19 at the time, and she did not want to go without someone; her friends were not available. (I was so complimented because when she had become a teenager, I could only go with her somewhere if I brought the credit card. I felt like she had readmitted me to the ranks of the socially acceptable.)

So I went to Weight Watchers. In a group of 80, sometimes I was the only man there. I think every man needs to attend Weight Watchers to discover some amazing things about women. I discovered something many others have, something I half-suspected—weight reduction is not about fat. It is a lot deeper than the surface of the skin. Sometimes I was so surprised by what I heard that I would gasp or laugh out loud, which would bring me an elbow in the ribs from my daughter.

The lecturers would talk about emotional eating as opposed to merely eating. They would share how people would become enslaved to food due to unaddressed inner issues. This combination of inner pain and eating as a pleasure would set up strong compulsions. One young mother volunteered this story. "My young daughter," she said, "was having a birthday party so I made a cake. The cake was half-eaten, so I wrapped it in plastic wrap, and then aluminum foil, and put it in the trash can outside. After doing that I put dirty diapers over the cake. A half hour later, I went back, dug through the dirty diapers, got the cake, and brought it inside. I unwrapped the foil, took off the plastic wrap, and ate the whole thing."

There is more going on in that person than hunger. She has been trained to deal with inner pain through food. How robot-like can that become? Another mother described how she received a phone call that her child had just been taken to the emergency room, and could she get there as soon as possible? She jumped into her car and sped toward the hospital. On the drive she stopped at a 7-11, picked up a box of donuts, and ate them on the way to the hospital. Did she love her child? Of course—that was the reason for the burst of fear and anxiety. But she had become addictively trained to deal with stress by eating. Even in the face of her own love for her child, she still robotically had to eat—even though her daughter was in danger and eating a dozen donuts while driving at high speed also endangered her own life.

Rules, Anxiety, and Addictions

At Weight Watchers, I lost about 25 pounds and won four red ribbons. (For every five pounds you lose, you get a red ribbon.) The woman who tracked my weight said, "You are doing really well—why not share with the group how you are doing this?" I was embarrassed, and I thought the women would resent me because I was a typical male who could roll the pounds off.

But there was another reason I didn't want to share. That reason was that *I did not care about my weight loss.* I was at Weight Watchers because I loved my daughter. Of all things, she wanted my company! Sure I was overweight, but it was not a big deal to me. So with the simple reminder to eat less, I did, and I lost weight. My great secret was my indifference! I did not have feelings of worthlessness and rejection driving me on the inside. Since I had no underlying negative mood, the temptation to overeat was very easy to push aside.

Here is the great irony: *The women's very anxiety about losing weight empowered and enhanced the desire to eat.* They needed the comfort of food and the mild chemical changes that food often brought to deal with that anxiety and worthlessness. Their will power was easily pushed aside by the turbo-driven desire for food. They were canoeing in the swamp of worthlessness, and the creature from the Black Lagoon, desire for food, snatched them.

The women needed to be indifferent and they were not. Many were in pain over their appearance, and many more were in pain for a lot of other reasons. But to them it was a big deal and a matter of anxiety. Weight Watchers was a great illustration of the "neurotic paradox": The more we know and are concerned about some appetite, the more powerful that appetite becomes.

The Guilt-and-Shame Brand of Christianity

Just as Weight Watchers can powerfully elevate women's anxiety, church also, believe it or not, can make the mood cycle even worse. Two of the most powerful emotions in the world are guilt and shame. And far too often many churches end up specializing in bringing those emotions into the lives of their attendees.

Take the situation of Ann. She is already struggling with the misuse of prescription drugs because of unaddressed emotional pain in her life. She is lonely because her children have left home and she and her husband argue all the time. (Incidentally, the largest group of people who misuse prescription drugs are women in their 40s.) She desperately wants to have a better marriage, and she wants to befriend other people, but she is too embarrassed to because she might have to talk about how deeply lonely she really is.

Ann regularly goes to church and hears that Christians should not use the crutch of antidepressants and medicines, and that a good Christian wife should be obedient to her husband and respect him. Those comments by the preacher add guilt to the misery she is already in. Then she goes further down the emotional spiral because in addition to her loneliness, hurt, and frustration, she now has added to it guilt over her wrongdoing and shame over the weaknesses she has.

This sort of thing sadly happens time after time after time to many believers. Many churches teach aggressively that Christ died to take away human sin so people can be right with God and be guilt-free. Yet to an extent that is tragic—because in the face of what they preach, many churches truly run on guilt and shame. If there is any institution that should have members who do not feel guilty and have a breezy confidence about their relationship with God, it should be the church. Such, sadly, is not the case.

When a person already has painful emotions within, it does not help to add guilt and shame to that mix. Over the years I have worked with people who have struggled with addiction, and one of the principles I have learned is that addicts swim in shame. Their lives are secretive and are built on mountains of lies. Guilt is also their constant companion. It's as if their life is built emotionally around a set of old-fashioned car brakes. Drum brakes work by an inner set of metal pads pushing up against an outer rim. The brake pads are the negative moods, and the outer rim is guilt and shame. As they push against each other, the resulting friction not only creates heat, it completely stops the life from going forward toward godliness.

Negative Emotions from Rules

Paul described this reality in Romans 7. There he explained how rules do not work. Neither human rules nor God's law has the power to tame sin within. In fact, they make it worse. "For when we were in the flesh, the moods (passions) which belonged to particular sins *which were through the Law* were continually energizing our bodily members to produce fruit for death" (verse 5). This is a deeply surprising insight. Rules that Christians naively think will help actually do the opposite. What do the rules of the Law produce? They produce guilt, shame, and worthlessness. These powerful moods energize the members of the body to produce death in the person's life. The members of the body already contain desire and appetite, but add to it the pain of guilt and shame, and sin has all the power it needs to control the life.

> *Guilt and shame inflame the mood cycle and pour gasoline on the flames of the works of the flesh and addictions.*

Notice also that the verse mentions "the moods (passions) which belonged to particular sins." Paul saw a direct connection between the moods, or passions, that inhabit our hearts and the sinful acts that the flesh produces. When the heart is regularly lambasted with rules and laws—"shoulds"—the spiritual life soon will fall apart. It is like Weight Watchers with eternal stakes. The stakes are not pounds to be added but souls to be lost or gained, holiness to be lived. At Weight Watchers everybody ended up preoccupied with losing weight and keeping the rules measured out by calories. At church many often end up not occupied with the grace of God and the energy that the Spirit provides, but preoccupied with not doing wrong and keeping the rules meted out as the preacher rides his latest "holy hobbyhorse."

Churches can with very good intentions turn themselves into hothouse nurseries for sins. Just turn the temperature up by repeatedly emphasizing what Christians have to do, supply a lot of shame for those who can't quite manage to do what's right, and the results will be directly opposite to what the preachers expect. Guilt and shame inflame the mood cycle and pour gasoline on the flames of the works of the flesh and addictions.

The recovery movement often passes out a small card with the word *guilt* written in black on it. Around the word is a red circle with a red line going across the word "guilt." The card means *no guilt*. The recovery movement has known for a long time that guilt makes addiction worse. In order for addiction to be beaten, the person has to step out of sin and shame. And what is true with the addiction cycle is true of its twin sister, the mood cycle.

⟿ ⟿ ⟿

How can we change what we have seen? How can we help this downward mood cycle? We have seen that negative emotions can take on a life of their own and severely damage people. We have also seen that these can empower and inflame appetites within us to produce works of the flesh or various types of addictive behaviors. We have also seen that the church can make things worse by overemphasizing rules and laws so that the powerful passions or moods of guilt, shame, and worthlessness are added to the mix.

Several years ago Adrianne, our daughter, brought a dog home. In the first week we had Teddy (as we named him), all he did was run around our sofa. He never stopped except to sleep. If anyone got close to him, he would bark and run. If anyone in the home raised an arm, he would bark and bare his teeth. Even after a few years, if he was out of his cage in the garage for more than an hour, he would go to the door and bark until we put him out there. He was too nervous to stay in the house.

Teddy had obviously been abused. He lived in a world where threats were everywhere. It took him years (a large part of a dog's life) and a lot of affection and work to get him to the point where he could relax some. As dog owners all we could do was change his environment and treat him with affection. Teddy could do very little for himself. He had no control over the experiences, sights, and reactions from the past that were controlling him.

Many of us inhabit a world similar to that of an abused animal. But we have an advantage that Teddy didn't have. We are not dogs. We can change the pictures from the past. We can step out of guilt and shame so that the emotional effects of rules and the law will not trap us. We can be free of the mood cycle.

When our heart pictures change, it is like being transported to a new land, a marvelous land of repose and comfort, a place where the heart does not have to be anxious about food, drink, and where to live. The land has a King who cares for its inhabitants, and when something hurtful happens, He brings benefit out of it in the short term and the long term.

Best of all, this land is a place of happy and healthy emotions. Peace, or tranquility, is the most common emotion. Relationships are loving and deeply affectionate. People do things for the King out of joy and not guilt.

The world of past pictures and experiences can be left behind. As we will see in more detail in part 2, we can choose new pictures for our hearts and can believe those pictures to be biblically true. And we can address these things because the Bible contains the resources for us to do so.

3

Are Emotions
Christian?

I WAS YOUNG, 22 AT THE TIME. It was late in the morning in San Francisco, and I had just left a wonderful seminary class that was exciting, interesting, and stimulating. I was walking downhill on Geary Street in the direction of Van Ness and downtown. Coming toward me was an attractive blond. The young woman's face was covered with one of the happiest expressions I'd ever seen—simply glowing with joy.

The thought leaped into my mind, *Ask her why she's so happy!* Instantly another thought jumped out: *I wish I was as happy as she is.* With that another one popped out: *You should be as happy as she is because you are a Christian, especially since you've just left a great theology class.*

A quick shot of shame went through me as I recognized I envied her. I'm not a shy person, but now I was embarrassed. If I asked why she was so happy, I would be asking to find out for myself how *I* could become as happy. *I'm a Christian,* I told myself. *I'm supposed to be happy!* I did not want to admit that a happy stranger with a wonderful smile could so quickly reduce me to a state of envy.

I never did ask her. I don't know what she would have answered. But it was in late-60's San Francisco, so she could have said that her joy came from a drug she had just taken—or perhaps she had just got engaged or got a big raise in pay. Thirty years later, I wish I had asked her. Now I would have because Christianity is meeting my deep emotional needs.

I think all of us Christians assume that knowing God and believing the Bible should meet our deep emotional needs. We say we are loved by the God who created the universe, and that the Bible contains all the truth we need for life and godliness. So why aren't all of us deeply happy?

Let's take another look at the diagram I introduced in chapter 1 so we can start exploring this question.

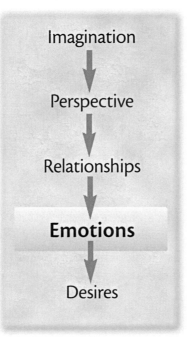

As we noted in chapter 2, Christians often assume that a life of godliness is just a matter of dealing with sinful acts and perhaps the desires that lead to them. We need to "work our way back up the chain," though. Personalized pictures of the truth within our imagination can affect everything down the line in our lives. But on our way to understanding how this works, we need to spend some time understanding emotions.

Misunderstanding Emotions

The church is now taking emotions seriously and valuing them, but it still appears not to know what to do with them. For this reason, major misunderstandings occur:

- ❧ *God is misunderstood.* Much confusion exists over God's own emotions, especially His love. Because of this, the church is neck-deep in confusion over God's character and His work of saving people. If we get the emotions of God straight, however, we can also get our own emotions right.

- ❧ *The Bible is misunderstood* because God is misunderstood. The Scriptures are treated like a book of information, a spiritual encyclopedia.

We're going to spend much of this chapter clearing these misconceptions out of the way so we can move toward emotional health.

A Hunger to Feel

Under the ceaseless activism of evangelicals is a deep and widespread hunger to have their emotions touched and involved in their faith, and to *feel* God's love and desire for them and His enjoyment of them. Evangelicals, whether they are the more

Bible-based or the more experienced-based, when scratched will bleed a strong desire to be emotionally fulfilled.

Two years before my walk down Geary Street, I was still in college. One evening I was talking to a woman about Pentecostalism and the Charismatic movement. I listened to her describing how wonderful it was to have a mighty work of the Holy Spirit going on in a person's life. I noticed the way emotions were described: They appeared to be something like an injectable fluid. For her, it appeared that the Holy Spirit simply dumped good feelings into a person's heart—you got baptized in the Spirit and the result was blissful happiness ever after.

I realize this is a vast oversimplification of what Pentecostals say, but that was the impression I was receiving. I simply responded to the woman that I was finding some wonderful truths in the book of Ephesians. Those truths were making me feel very happy and very loved by God. The experience was meaningful to me and brought joy. Almost instantly she left what she was trying to "sell" and began to tell me how frustrating her life was and how she wished it were different. When the "sales job" of Christianity is set aside, unhappy hearts surface among the "sales force."

The Pentecostal and Charismatic movement does emphasize how important it is for the Christian to have a rich emotional life. That's healthy. It also emphasizes that Christianity has to be more than just learning more Bible information. That's also healthy. However, over the years, as I have become friends with many Pentecostals and Charismatics, I have seen that they have the same emotional needs and deficiencies as their more Bible-oriented brethren.

Emotional Malnourishment

Here's an example that gives a snapshot of the latter case. Our nonprofit organization works with Campus Crusade. We put on seminars for and counsel their staff and students. What we have found over and over again is that the students and staff are serious and dedicated but malnourished emotionally. Quite a bit of what they do is on the level of sheer blind obedience.

When I talk privately to Christian students who are involved with this fine evangelical organization, I always ask if the student has a deep sense, or any sense, of being loved by God. Can he or she feel the love of God? Almost always the answer is no. Their emotional gas tank is empty, but they keep going. If the student is male, the answer is simply no; if the student is female, the no is given with tears.

Often it is the same with the staff. Mike is a campus director on the West Coast. Once he met with a group of Christian businessman to discuss his work with Crusade. One of the businessmen asked, "Why would non-Christians want what you have?" At the time, deep within himself, he was not sure they would. Mike never actually told me what he answered, but he did share with me the dialogue going on within himself. He thought that the non-Christians needed what he had to keep them from going to hell, but they did not need the lack of happiness and the religious drivenness that was his life. He said, "I wasn't sure that the good news was good news for me at all."

Mike's situation was not unusual. Many who serve God diligently in parachurch organizations and within the church itself are running on fumes and not on an emotionally robust Christianity. Their leaders have told them that obedience is everything, and that Jesus has suffered and so they should also. But they forget that Jesus said, "My peace I leave with you, not as the world gives" (John 14:27). He told us not to be troubled or afraid. He was saying, in effect, that emotional vibrancy can exist in the midst of suffering!

A Reflection of Our Culture

But the search for joy and peace is present not only among those who profess Christianity. Christians reflect the same longing found in the nonchurched community at large. The culture as a whole does not know what to do with emotions, and emotional health and happiness are major issues.

We live in a world where everyone wants to feel better and have healthy emotions. Turn on the TV, and from *Dr. Phil* to *Law and Order* emotions are swirling and powerful. But when you come to the management, maintenance, and improvement of our emotional life, the consistent message is to encourage us to see a doctor for a prescription. The general impression is given that if you want to feel really good, fall passionately in love with someone—or if you are feeling bad, take a pill.

For close to 75 years Americans have been told that counseling cures. In the United States we have had three generations participate in the therapeutic revolution. Millions upon millions have been in therapy, participated in small groups, and attended recovery meetings. In ways that has helped some, but as the culture's means of obtaining joy, it appears not to have worked or met the promised expectations. Our divorce rate is through the roof. People are not happy together, and they are not happy alone. The demand for counseling is so intense and widespread that health insurance companies are now regularly refusing to pay for long-term counseling. So what is now substituting for it is medication.

The most reliable approach our culture offers to emotional difficulty is to chemically alter people. Taking a pill makes some sense because God has made us as a walking, talking, moving sack of chemicals. God has put within this walking, talking sack of chemicals, however, the capacity for deep and profound changes to take place through a relationship with Him.

How Do We Understand God's Emotions?

Over and against our culture's medication-based approach, Christians rightly emphasize the central place of humanity's relationship with God. In Christianity the great message is that God is love and that He has acted in love in the sending of His Son.

But here's where we run into the first huge misunderstanding of God's emotions. At this point, in many Christian circles a strange twist happens. The twist goes something like this: Since God has acted in love by the sending of His Son, then love must be an act of the will that results in an act of sacrifice. Love, then, is defined as a decision of the will and an act of sacrifice.

Everything just said is partially true, and that's why it's confusing. But it leaves the most important aspect out: Love is a passionate delight between persons. The heart of love is the passion of one person for another. (Misunderstanding God's love is such a serious problem among Christians that we're going to spend all of chapter 9 letting the Bible's truth destroy many of the typical misconceptions. What I'm saying here is just a foretaste of what's coming!)

It is an utter eye-opener as to what is going on in evangelicalism when I tell people that God likes them and could shed tears over their heartaches. For many Christians that is new news. Many do not act like it is also great news. Instead they act confused. The teaching they've heard, which says *agape* love is just a decision of the will and an act of sacrifice, treats emotions just like they are the exhaust coming out of the engine.* In fact, biblically emotions *are* the engine!

---

* What is odd is that those who make a point of emphasizing that love is just an act of the will often make a great point that God's anger and wrath is real and should be taken with dead earnestness. The question is, If His love is just intellectual and an act of the will, why are His anger and wrath not just intellectual? We should not pick and choose God's emotional states. If His anger is real and emotional, let's make His *agape* love that too!

Why the Cross?

Because God's love is misunderstood, His atonement—Jesus' saving work on the cross—is also misunderstood. Having talked to thousands of Christians over the years, I've found that the misconceptions are numerous. One of the major ones is that the atonement is thought to make us lovable. In fact, though, God's emotional delight, or *agape* love, preceded the atonement. As amazing as it may seem, He does deeply love the unlovely, and because He does, He can come to the rescue of the sin-marred. (We walked through a picture of this truth at the end of chapter 1.)

Or let's look at this a different way. Many Christians seem surprised that God the Father can love and like people. They have received the impression that God is a big blob of noble, disinterested love who chooses to love and sacrifice because that is just what nobility does. *Who* a person is does not matter. What matters is that God is morally obligated to love. It is His job description.

> His plan to save people started with His individual love for individual persons.

That is not the way love works. You cannot *will* passionate delight or love. Like the love among the members of the Trinity, love for persons flows only unbidden. Love exists only among persons and in relationships. And because God loves individual people—in Christ or not in Christ—He has brought about the atonement. Notice in Ephesians 2:4-5 how salvation flows from God's love and, as a result, makes us objects of His deliverance.

> God, being rich in mercy, because of His great passionate love with which He passionately loved us, even when we were corpses in our trespasses, made us alive together with Christ (by grace you have been permanently saved).

Even when we were spiritually dead, abundant mercy and love was in God's heart for us. His plan to save people started with His individual love for individual persons.

How Do We Understand the Bible?

If we are misunderstanding God's emotions (and we'll go over this more extensively in the next chapter), included in that we will misunderstand what the Book of God, the Bible, says about emotions. I was teaching a spiritual life seminar at a church in Palo Alto, California. In the second row of the auditorium was seated a very serious-looking man who looked like he was from India but who turned out to be from Oregon. As I spoke his brow wrinkled, and his eyes squinted more and more tightly. The more concerned he looked, the more I could not help but notice him.

During the break in a lecture, he came up to me and said, "You keep saying that one of the goals of Christianity is to produce an emotional richness in our lives. That is not what I have been taught. Are you sure that you are right?"

I thought it would be unwise to say, "Sure I'm right." Instead I asked him a series of questions. We were studying Colossians 2, so I asked him to turn there. I pointed out verses 1 through 3.

> I want you to know how great a struggle I have on your behalf, and for those who are at Laodicea, and for all those who have not personally seen my face, that their hearts may be encouraged, they being knit together in love, and unto all riches of the full assurance of understanding, that they may know the mystery of God, Christ.

As he and I were looking at the page, I asked, "When hearts are encouraged, is that something that just occurs in the mind, or is that something that can be seen in the face?"

He looked uncomfortable and said, "Probably it will show up on the face."

I asked, "Will the person look happy or sad?"

Looking like he was sucking on a lemon, he said, "They probably will look happy."

"Is happy an emotion?"

"It is."

Then, I said, notice that one of Paul's goals is that the believers should have their hearts knitted together in love. "When believer's hearts are knitted together in love, is that something that has emotions with it, or is it all mental?"

He saw what was coming and said quietly, "It's emotional; and people can see it."

Continuing, I asked, where Paul wanted believers to come to a full assurance of understanding, is assurance something that affects the emotions? He replied that the emotions are affected. When people are confident, I asked, "Does it show on the face?" He said it certainly did.

The strange thing was that his face did not reveal any happiness about God's intent that we should be happy. Instead his brow was wrinkled and his face was serious. He then said, "If what you say is true—that emotions should be present in the life of the Christian and that they indicate how well Christianity is understood—then you are talking about a complete revolution from the emotionless Christianity that most of us are used to." I assured him that was exactly what I was saying.

I began the next part of the lecture by explaining my answer to him further. Many times people use an old-style train to describe Christianity. *Fact* is said to be the engine, *faith* is the tender with the coal, and *feelings* are the caboose. The caboose is often represented as being unimportant in the Christian life, but that is far from the truth. The caboose is attached to the train, and it must certainly arrive at the destination sooner or later. If it does not arrive, it may mean that the engine is detached or that no coal is in the tender! Emotions should and do play a major part in biblical Christianity. Feelings of confidence and hope prove the truth is accurately understood, faith is properly present, and the Spirit of God is at work.

Emotions and Biblical Truth

With regard to emotions, the Bible is misunderstood in a number of other ways. As I noted earlier, many people make the mistake of thinking that it is a spiritual encyclopedia, an information book. Too many Christians view the Bible as a text to be studied so as to prepare for a quiz show run by God—something like a divine Jeopardy game with big stakes. The Bible's goal is not the impartation of *information*, but true *integration*, wherein truth becomes instinct.

Let me underscore this point with an example. I participate in training pastors for ministry and Christian counselors for counseling. I have spent a significant part of my adult life giving tests on the Bible to ministry students, and I have found that answers on a paper test have yet to change anyone's life. Instead, I would love to offer an empathy exam.

Why? In the letter to the Colossians again, chapter 3 describes a spiritual life development process. The last step of the process is becoming a person of deep compassion. After working through what they were to do with what is going on inside with the desires, appetites, and moods, Paul told the Christians that a healthy goal for true spiritual development was to clothe themselves with compassion. The "therefore" at the beginning of verse 12 follows a process of searching and deeply relational prayer.

> Therefore, as God's chosen people, permanently holy and permanently loved, put on like clothing compassion, kindness, humility, gentleness, and patience.

Notice that Paul did not write to the Colossians telling them they needed to memorize what five things they were to clothe themselves with. Instead, he directed them through a process of coming to terms with what was going on in the inner life in such a way that the outer, relational life was characterized by compassion. The important thing was not the information, but the other-centered emotions.

The point of Christianity is not *knowing information about* God but *having the emotions of* God! The most common emotion of Christ in the Gospels is compassion.*

Scripture *memorization* is not the goal, but Scripture *integration*. (There is a story about rabbis that some of them had the Old Testament scrolls so well memorized that if you stuck a pin through a scroll, they could tell you every word the pin went through. Sadly, it was the same rabbis who could not recognize God in Christ.)

Probably the most important use of emotions with regard to the Bible is often overlooked. The principle is as follows: *Emotions do not authenticate truth, but emotions do authenticate our understanding and integration of truth.* Emotions will not authenticate the truth of Christ's resurrection, but our emotions will authenticate that we understand the *implications* of the resurrection. Emotions have a profoundly important function in the Bible—they show us that we are understanding and integrating truth. They will show us whether we have a healthy relationship with God.

Let's illustrate this with an example about prayer. Philippians tells us that it is not the watch—the amount of time we spend—

---

* See Matthew 9:36; 14:14; 15:32; 20:34; Mark 1:41; 6:34; 8:2; Luke 7:13.

that determines the quality and effectiveness of our prayer life. Rather, our emotions do! Notice what it says:

> Stop being anxious about anything, but in relationship to everything making you nervous by prayer and supplication with thanksgiving let your specific requests be made known to God. And the peace of God, which surpasses all comprehension, shall guard your hearts and your thought processes in Christ Jesus (4:6-7).

What is supposed to prompt a life of prayer is not what time it is, but our anxiety. That emotion tells us that we should go talk to our "Dad" in heaven. He does not want His children living with anxiety. Instead, we are to share the anxious threats with Him, ask for specific help, and thank Him that He is always greater than any problem that assaults us. We are able to tell we have been effective in our prayers by the peace that results, not the amount of time that passes. This tranquility is so powerful that it positively guards the heart from the assaults of fear.

I strongly suspect more people have memorized Philippians 4:6-7 than have experienced it. In sum, though, the purpose of Paul's exhortation is to produce a certain kind of peaceful experience. We, then, are to pray until we are peaceful. It is not the time, but the emotional result, that matters.

Emotions in the Bible's Teaching

Not only are the Bible and the Bible's teachings on emotions misunderstood, but as a further result, the impact of specific Scriptures is not understood. For example, one of the primary points in the story of the woman at the well in John 4 often is missed. Jesus asked a Samaritan woman for a drink of water, for which they shared a mutual need. He then told her if she actually knew who it was talking with her and would ask Him, He would place a deep spring of water and refreshment within her and that would spring up to eternal life (verse 10).

To no one else in the Gospel of John did Jesus say such a thing. He seemed to be greatly interested in making a difference in her emotional life. Often when people exhibit suspicion in adult life ("why are you, a Jew, asking water from me?"—verse 9), when their emotions are damaged or nonexistent (indicated by Jesus' words, "I will place a spring within you"—verse 13), and when they volunteer limited information ("I don't have a husband"—verse 17), it is because of great stress in their background. Sure enough, Jesus informed her of the great stress in her life: She had had five husbands, and the man she was with now was not her husband. Christ went on to tell her that a Father in heaven wanted to have a spiritual relationship with her (4:21-24) so as to reparent her. Out of that relationship, the emotional damage in her life would be repaired.

John 4 revolves around the image of water as a metaphor for the emotional refreshment Jesus can bring into the life. Out of that story we should see that one of Jesus' divine missions was to enrich our emotional life. Just as in John 4, emotions are talked about and addressed throughout Scripture. One of the strategies of Satan is always to make us blind to the obvious. The obvious point in the Bible is that a rich and positive emotional life is there for the taking by the child of God.

The Church's Unhealthy Substitutes

Tragically, when the rich emotional aspects of the Christian life are overlooked, in unhealthy churches other emotions are frequently used to motivate Christians instead. The most powerful force to galvanize a church is the emotions of the fruit of the

Spirit: love, joy, and peace. If, however, the leadership does not understand how to bring a biblical emotional life to a church, they will resort to other emotions because they realize that without the drive of the emotional, people will simply not move.

Instead of spiritual fruit, the leaders will use the moods of the flesh. Guilt, shame, and worthlessness will be used like whips to motivate. And when emotions are misunderstood, minimized, and misused, the fallout will not only involve emotions themselves—other important biblical truths will be affected.

The Fallout from Motivation by Guilt

Take, for instance, our faith walk. If Christians do not use the presence of the fruit of the Spirit—peace and love—to authenticate that they have a correct understanding of truth, they often end up thinking (almost by default) that *guilt* should be the normal emotion of the Christian life. In fact, we have entire generations of Christians who have been trained to feel more comfortable with guilt than peace.

When guilt is made normal, other parts of the spiritual life suffer. Our faith walk suffers, and unbelief becomes rampant. Because this is such a common issue in the church, let's take a moment to see how guilt and unbelief play off each other. Read this verse first without an important change.

> When he asks, he must believe and not *doubt*, because he who *doubts* is like a wave top of the sea, blown and tossed by the wind (James 1:6).

Now let me change the word *doubt* to some words that more accurately reflect the Greek language of the New Testament.

> When he asks, he must believe and not *continually reexamine*,
> because he who *continually reexamines* is like a wave top of
> the sea, blown and tossed by the wind.

The way *doubt* is used here does not mean a refusal to believe (as it is often defined). *Doubting* means to continually go back and recheck to make sure that what God said is true and that all the conditions of trusting have been met. Faith is when we say, "I will trust God and wait on Him to keep His Word." Faith knocks the ball back into God's court and then waits on Him to do something. Faith does not stand there and ask, "Did I use the right technique, the right swing...did I breathe in or breathe out at the right time...was I sincere when I swung...did I get it over the net?"

Working Off the Guilt

Faith relaxes into the promises of God; unbelief relaxes about nothing. Faithlessness, or doubt, is an endless questioning; faith is a calm waiting. But if we have come to sincerely believe that guilt is the normal Christian state, then every time we exercise genuine faith and peace results, we will think something is wrong. We will go on to reexamine ourselves—doubt, in other words— and eventually we will find the guilt we feel we need.

Guilt like this inflames the mood cycle, and with the inflaming of the mood cycle, addictive behavior and works of the flesh appear. I suspect the state of workaholism among many members of the church is directly related to this. Workaholism is an acceptable evangelical vice. Often noticed with suspicion by those outside the church, workaholism or endless church activity is praised by many within the church. Sadly, for many it may simply be activity to lessen guilt.

Negative Emotions Do Have a Role

Before we move on to the positive emotions of the Christian life in chapter 4, let's look at one more thing. One question that may have come up in your mind is, "If guilt, shame, and anxiety are not to be our primary emotions, what purpose do they serve?"

Let me share a story that I created to illustrate the usefulness of anxiety, guilt, and shame. All of us know who the seven dwarves are in the story of Snow White: Sleepy, Sneezy, Doc, Grumpy, Bashful, Dopey, and Happy. Well, there are actually three other dwarves: Anxiety, Shame, and Guilt.

Snow White was lost a second time in the forest, and she wandered for many hours. This time she was not escaping from the jealous queen, she was looking for her Father's House. She took a short nap, and she was awakened by a tapping on her shoulder. Anxiety, Shame, and Guilt, the three dwarves, were standing over her. She asked them for the direction to her Father's House. They said that they knew where it was and would take her there.

> *When emotions are discounted within the church culture, then anxiety, guilt, and shame get substituted for love, joy, and peace.*

As they went briskly along, the dwarves did not whistle as they walked; they groaned and moaned, as was their habit. Such moaning and groaning was why the other seven dwarves did not like to keep the unhappy threesome around. Not even Grumpy wanted them around.

Soon they came to the Father's House. They stopped at the steps before the door. At that point, Snow White told the dwarves they could not come into the Father's House. She said that she was happy to have Anxiety, Guilt, and Shame to awaken her heart and lead her to the Home of the Father. But they could never come into the Home, because the Father never would want His children to experience Shame, Guilt, and Anxiety in His presence. He would not want her to bring them inside.

Putting this story into other words, our normal spiritual emotions are to be peace, joy, and love. Anxiety, guilt, and shame are to be short-term emotions that remind us to sort things out with our Father.

- ⚘ Short-term guilt means we are to confess and make things right with the Father and so restore our peace.

- ⚘ Short-term anxiety means a threat is out there that we need to deal with in prayer.

- ⚘ Short-term shame means we have fallen short and need to go to the Father with that issue.

But when emotions are discounted within the church culture, then anxiety, guilt, and shame get substituted for love, joy, and peace; activities and goals get substituted for the fruit of the Spirit; and we end up misrepresenting God and His Word.

⚘ ⚘ ⚘

I started this chapter by talking about meeting a pretty young woman on the streets of San Francisco whose happy appearance reduced me to envy. Now let me close with a story of another woman, whom I met on the streets of Berkeley, California. I was working at the Graduate Theological Union Library in Berkeley doing some research. (Berkeley, as you probably know, is a very liberal town, and the theological schools in Berkeley are almost all very liberal.)

I came out of the library to take a breather and stretch my legs. This time a rather large, not very happy-looking woman came walking toward me. She looked less happy than the grim reaper! Suddenly she shouted, "You are going to hell! You need to repent—and when you do, attend Faith Baptist Church in Richmond!" Then she kept on walking.

All of this happened so fast that I was shocked and speechless. Nothing about her demeanor was an argument for the truth. She looked unhappy, and she acted rude. I had no desire to ask her about anything—except what in her life had led her to become a human evangelistic missile. I am sure she was completely sincere, but her message was flatly contradicted by her emotional state. When our emotions are not the fruit of the Spirit, we may well end up deeply misrepresenting our Savior, who has rescued us to bring us into His joy.

Emotions, good or bad, have a place in our lives and God's plan. Our emotions are part of God's way of keeping us healthy. We need to know how the pleasurable and painful ones work and what they mean. Teaching us to understand our emotions is one of the great goals of the Bible.

But emotions have a greater significance than just as a means of supporting spiritual health. We shall see what that is in the next chapter. Emotions have a wonderful source and a great mission.

4

You Can't
Live Without Them

$\text{\textbrokenbar}$ $\text{\textbrokenbar}$ $\text{\textbrokenbar}$

A WHILE BACK I HAD THE MORE frightening than interesting experience of having my right eye operated on. The procedure was complicated, so the operation was at a hospital. While I was waiting outside the operating room on a gurney, an anesthesiologist came over to check on me. We ended up in a conversation. I told him that having a series of eye problems had led me to appreciate how wonderfully our two eyes worked together to create the sense of depth. I did not want to lose that, I said.

Then his face brightened up and he said, "Isn't evolution fantastic? Because a million years ago we had one eye in the middle of our heads, and then it migrated down to our face, and on the way it split in half." Gesturing, he placed two hands together on the top of his head and slid each hand down to each eye. "That's how we got two eyes," he stated.

Please understand I had been in pain for months and had experienced high levels of stress. I am not normally as rude as I will now appear.

"That is so stupid," I replied, "that I'm almost *forced* into believing God did it." However, the anesthesiologist got the best of the argument because shortly thereafter I was unconscious.

Eyesight, and the sense of depth perception that having two eyes gives us, are just a couple of the wondrous things about being human. Our bodies are repositories of wonder. Within our frame is an unimaginably complex set of abilities. From whistling a tune to thinking up the splitting of the atom, we are fearfully and wonderfully made. Yet the greatest wonder of all is that all of this is expressed by a walking pile of chemical and electrical activity. This is so wonderful that it makes the existence of God reasonable.

Among all these different wonders inside of us is a whole world of appetites, imagination, and emotions. Though our emotions are inside of us and sometimes come from places deep within, that is not where they ultimately come from. The source of emotions is a surprising place—or more precisely, a Person. That Person is God.

Because we are emotional beings, we feel and want, relate and think. And since the Bible says we are made in God's image, we can look at ourselves and be certain that He is an emotional being too. At the center of reality is a Being who feels, wants, relates, and thinks.

A Deeply Emotional God

In the Bible we are told very clearly that God is not physical, but we are also told very emphatically that He feels and thinks. The language of the Bible expresses it this way. He is *spirit,* and He has *soul.* The classic statement for the first is John 4:24: "God is spirit." The Greek construction emphasizes *spirit* as a quality. A way of translating the phrase would be, "God as to quality is spirit." *Spirit* implies self-awareness, reflection, and will—and also a non-physical existence. When one examines how the Hebrew word and Greek word for *spirit* are used, they are commonly connected to terms of reflection, intellect, and intention.

God is also described as having a soul. *Soul* implies sensation, feelings, and appetites. God has what can be described as a soul since He is a feeling being. Some erroneously take the language revolving around the word *soul* and almost turn it into some substance within God or man. However, *soul* is not a thing but a word that means we and God have the ability to feel and want. Notice how it is used to indicate feelings in the following verse.

> Yahweh said to me: "Even if Moses and Samuel were to stand before me, My soul would not go out to this people. Send them away from My presence! Let them go!" (Jeremiah 15:1).*

Yahweh was saying that He did not have any sympathy for or desire to help the people. Notice how the word *soul* was connected to very strong feelings of dislike! In the next verse the language gets even stronger.

> Your New Moon festivals and your appointed feasts My soul hates. They have become a burden to Me; I am weary of bearing them (Isaiah 1:14).

If God's soul has the capacity to strongly dislike, it follows that His soul must have the capacity to strongly like and enjoy. In a later part of Isaiah, God described His feelings about the future servant, the Lord Jesus Christ, who was predicted to appear.

> Here is My servant, whom I hold fast, My chosen one in whom My soul delights; I will put my Spirit on Him and He will bring justice to the nations (Isaiah 42:1).

---

* *Yahweh* is the personal name of God in the Old Testament, and it means "He who is."

We Reflect God's Having Emotions

The terms *soul* and *spirit* describe what God experiences within Himself. *Soul* implies that the person has appetites and emotions, while *spirit* implies that the person can reflect and be self-observing. That we are made in His image is the reason for our emotions and our thoughts. Men and women are similar to animals in having flesh, soul, and spirit,* but the critical difference is that we are made in the image of God.

Everything about us is a reflection of the divine: We are an analogy of the divine. Yes, we have a soul like God, but that is only a part of it. And indeed we have a spirit like God, but it is more than that. *Everything* about us is an insight into deity.

The Bible is not afraid of using powerfully emotional words and surprising terms for the depth of God's emotional life. Sometimes the language used of God's emotions is so concrete that modern Bible translators water them down or change them. For example, the old King James Version used the term *bowels*—our modern word *intestines*—for deep compassion. In the Greek in which the New Testament was written, the word *bowels*, or *intestines*, appeared. For example,

God's bowels of compassion are open to us (Luke 1:78).

No one anywhere believes that God has intestines, but the message of the verse must not be ignored. God has the capacity to be deeply touched within. The way we say it, is that He has "gut feelings." In the ancient world when someone was touched deeply, they would say that their intestines were moved. To emphasize how deeply God can connect with us, that language was used.

---

* See 1 Corinthians 2:11; Genesis 7:22; Ecclesiastes 3:21-22.

God in turn created us as deeply emotional beings. In the last day of the six days of creation in Genesis 1, He placed the animals on the land. In the very last part of that sixth day, He created humanity. Verse 26 needs to be observed carefully.

> Then God said, "Let us make man in our image, in our likeness, in order that they might rule over the fish of the sea and the birds of the air, over the livestock, over all the earth, and over all the creatures that move along the ground."

God's purpose in making humanity in His image was so that the planet might be ruled. The point is that the goal of man and woman was to fulfill a purpose. The Hebrew words actually mean "*in order that.*" They were created in the image of God *in order that* they might rule. They needed to be made in God's image and likeness, otherwise the rule would not be effective. The only way to find an adequate ruler was for God to create a regent like Himself. That is where emotions come in. Part of that image and likeness is not only the ability to think, it is also the ability to feel. God not only wanted a brilliant set of rulers, He also wanted a sensitive set of rulers—and that is the reason for emotions.

Genesis 1, with the creation of humanity, placed us in relationship to the world. But it was in Genesis 2 that God related the genders to one another and to Him and this comment was made.

> Then Yahweh God formed man of the dust of the ground, and breathed into his nostrils the breath of life; and man became a living soul (verse 7).

The man became a soul, or a living sensate being. It is interesting that the writer of Genesis could have said that Adam became a living spirit, or a living body, or a living man, but instead he said that Adam became a living *soul*. Another way of saying that is, Adam became a living, breathing bundle of emotions and desires. That is what a living soul is. We have emotions because we are made in God's image—and God made us that way!

The Promise of Christianity

When Jesus came to this earth, one of His missions was deeply emotional.

> These things have I spoken to you, in order that My joy may be among you, and your joy should be complete (John 15:11).

God has not only come to deliver us from our sins and bring us home to heaven. God has come to make us happy. The three Persons of the Trinity experience joy, and they want to bring us into that circle of joy and love.

Jennifer was a 19-year-old Chinese–American who had made a profession of faith. While in a church service she heard a preacher speak of God's love for the individual and how the cross expressed that love. As she listened a deep sense of affection from God and for God swept through her. She felt loved. With that everything changed, and nothing remained the same. The universe was a place where affection for her existed.

The next day she stood outside her house watching trees being blown by the wind. The leaves looked scintillating and different. She thought, *God made those trees and He made them for me. He loves me and those are His gifts to me!* That picture of being loved by God became the foundational experience of her adult life. Her life experiences oftentimes were hurtful and shaming. An abusive marriage came into her life like bitterly blown waves. Even so, those fierce waves always just crashed against the shoreline rocks of God's love. She told me that the experience of being loved by God became the refuge of her adult life. She had found emotional health.

Using Our Emotions in a Spiritual Way

As we noted, God as to His quality of existence is spirit. Now, no one can imagine that God is anything other than emotionally healthy. It follows that we need to use our emotions in a spiritual way in order to be healthy emotional beings. All this naturally leads to the question, What is emotional health, and what is the spiritual use of emotions?

> Christianity promises what pills attempt to provide.

I am going to argue that emotional health and spiritual health are the same. In fact, the more spiritually healthy you are, the more emotionally healthy you will be—because in reality they are the same. Let me share a story to underscore what I am saying.

"All my friends are taking them, so I want some antidepressants too," the patient demanded.

His doctor appeared confused. "Are you depressed?"

The patient replied, "Not at all, but if everyone is taking pills for mental health, shouldn't I?"

"Let me ask you some questions," the doctor said, puzzled. "Are you happy?"

"Yes."

"Is your marriage going all right?"

"Yes."

"Do you feel like your life is worthwhile?"

"Yes."

"Are you anxious about anything?"

"No, except I'm a little concerned about the parking meter outside."

"Are you in any physical pain?"

"No."

"Well, why on earth do you want antidepressants? They're just pills."

The patient said authoritatively, "I have heard that psychopharmaceuticals are the latest advance in medicine for helping our emotional and psychological health. I want some."

"Unfortunately," the doctor said, "you are not depressed, you feel worthwhile, you're happily married, and you are happy. Frankly, a pill might ruin that. In fact, you might consider giving seminars on how you ended up happy. I'm not happy. I'm divorced, and I'm taking Prozac. So tell me how you got into the shape that you're in!"

Many of us need to think through the implications of this story. Christianity promises what pills attempt to provide. For instance, the Old Testament word for peace is *shalom,* and it means more than just peace. *Shalom* means a sense of tranquility with deep feelings of well-being. That is what is promised in the Proverbs and the Psalms.

> Length of days, and years of life, and peace, or *shalom,* will they [the writer's words of wisdom] add to you (Proverbs 3:2).

> Yahweh will give strength to His people; Yahweh will bless His people with peace, or *shalom* (Psalm 29:11).

God Cares About Our Emotional Health

Part of the damage called by confusion concerning what the Bible says about God's emotions and our emotions is that we lose the truth that God is very much interested in our mental and emotional health. The spiritual person is the healthy person and the nice person. One of the sad things is that Christian spirituality has become divorced from the reality of people's lives. It is because information has been substituted for integration—and what words like peace, love, and joy pointed to has been defaced and reduced to meaninglessness. Word games have been substituted for reality.

The first step for emotional health for the Christian is to realize that emotions matter to God and to us. The Bible has always shown that God is concerned about the emotional state of His people. He does not want His people to be experiencing the torture of negative emotions. In fact, the Bible will attempt to encourage us by telling us that God is emotionally involved with us.

Many Bible-teaching churches, however, seem emotionless. I think one reason for this is that they are built on abstract bits of information that cannot reach us emotionally. If God is presented as a bland, impassive God and not the emotionally rich God of the Bible, the church will function as a college classroom instead of a living fellowship. God gave us emotions to use. As we have said, our emotions are analogous to His emotions. His were first. We are made in His image. We have emotions because He does.

God is indeed emotionally involved with us, but due to inaccurate Bible teaching many Christians have instinctively concluded that the God of the Bible is not emotionally involved with them. They're not even sure if He likes them. They just suppose He is neutral about everything.

But nothing could be further from the truth. The God of the Bible is passionately in love with each of us! He likes us! If you are a woman, He'd take you for a walk and a talk. If you are a man,

He'd go fishing with you. He is a lover of men and women. If you are discouraged, the God of the Bible would encourage you.

It's in the Bible!

The Bible teaches God's emotional involvement with us in an interesting way. For example, the book of Psalms tells us to consider an emotionally healthy dad and how he relates to his children. In Psalm 103:13 it says this:

> Just as a father has deep emotional involvement with his children, so Yahweh has compassion, or deep emotional involvement, on those who have a respect for Him. For He Himself personally knows our frame. He remembers that we are but dust.

David used the model of a healthy human father for how God relates. "Just as a father" implies a good father. David says that the Lord has compassion like a father. Did you notice how the Bible went from how our emotions work, such as the compassion of a healthy dad, to how God's emotions work?

The New Testament does the same thing: it works from how our emotions and relationships work to how God's emotions and relationships work. Notice in the Gospel of Matthew how Christ goes from our feelings about our children to how God feels about us. This again will show that God is concerned with our emotions and He really does want to "emotionally connect" with us.

> What sort of man is there among you, when his son shall ask him for a loaf, he won't give him a stone, will he? Or if he shall ask for a fish, he will not give him a snake, will he? You then, being evil, know how to give good gifts to your children, how much more shall your Father who is in heaven

give what are beneficial things to those who ask Him! (Matthew 7:9-11).

Christ in Matthew described how parents will not give a snake to a child when the child asked for bread, or a stone if the child asked for a fish. Our feelings of sympathy and love for our children, he implied, prompt us to be kind and caring to our own. Since we are fallen creatures and yet we need to be kind to our own, does it not follow that God will be superior in affection and loyalty? The text and the culture of Christ's time would presuppose that. Christ then says that those emotions should lead to the thought that God indeed will be *more* generous. *Even our "fallen" emotions can tell us something about God.* Because we have caring emotions, Christ is implying God has too. Since we are made in the image of God, we can either start from ourselves to learn something about God, as Christ does in this story, or we can start out with what the Bible says about God.

Jesus' Concern for Our Emotions

It is not only God the Father who has a concern about our emotional life. Jesus has a deep concern also about our emotional life. Jesus realized that people will often avoid dealing with the issues of emotions and the heart by religious activism. He wanted to make sure that we do not substitute religious activism for the gift of a rich emotional life.

A perfect example of this is in a passage about God's gentleness in Matthew 11:28-30. Jesus said,

> You are ordered to come to Me, all you who are worn out and overburdened, and I will give you rest. Take My yoke upon you, and be discipled by Me, for I am gentle and humble in heart; and you shall find refreshment for your souls. For my yoke is kindly and my burden is light.

Christ is speaking to people who have been deceived by a religious system that has worn them down and exhausted them. The word *gentle* used by Christ to describe Himself means to be emotionally mild. When we meet Jesus in heaven, we won't be consumed by the intensity of a divine fanaticism, but we will meet a Person of mild emotions. He is an easygoing God. When we talk to Him, He will set us at ease. Feelings of total acceptance will force open the doors of our hearts so that the most open communication we will ever experience will occur. Every moment will feel like we have just come from a swim in a refreshing spring.

Heaven is relaxing because the God of heaven is other-centered. He values others so much that, as a good host, He wants those in heaven to feel special. I can imagine what might run through a person's mind after meeting Jesus face-to-face for the first time. I can see the confusion in this person's eyes as they think, *I can't believe it! Jesus didn't make one demand of me. He kept telling me to relax. I expected Him to recruit me as an usher as soon as I arrived. But He didn't. He just said to relax. What a strange God. This isn't like church at all.* Ironically, for many Christians the condition of being weighed down and burdened sounds like their life in the local church.

Kim (whom we met in the preface) believed that the God of the Bible was a score-keeping, critical God who was perpetually upset over every little thing she did wrong. When she learned that God was easygoing, she relaxed. "If He can relax," she said, "so can I." She thought to herself that such a God could even be likable. From having a God who reminded her of her mom, she went to a God who was a Person in His own right!

Jesus says He is emotionally mild and humble in heart. I strain over that phrase. How can the Creator of the universe possibly be humble in heart? Yet He is, because He will not impose Himself on anyone. He will not even impose heaven on anyone. Hell exists because God refuses to impose heaven. The forbidden Tree of the Knowledge of Good and Evil existed because God refused to impose the Garden of Eden on anyone. He gave Adam and Eve a choice even about Paradise.

The Carnal Use of Emotions

A healthy spiritual relationship with God generates a matrix of very powerful emotions: love, joy, and peace. The Christian emotions should be qualitatively superior to what is in the world, but they still are forceful emotions. As we relate to the Father God, the Holy Spirit relates to us and gives us the emotional richness we need to sustain a powerful Christian life. Spiritual Christians are happy Christians, and happy Christians are spiritual Christians.

The opposite is also true. Emotional unhealthiness is spiritual unhealthiness, or as the Bible calls it, *carnality* (fleshliness). There are thousands of examples in the Scriptures, but let's look at one from Isaiah. The last third of this book has a phrase, repeated three times, that speaks of the condition of those who do not know our God.

> There is no peace, or *shalom*, says Yahweh, to the wicked (Isaiah 48:22).

There is no *shalom*, or sense of well-being, for the wicked. Deep within, pain and distress exist. The Bible assumes that a person outside of Christ does not have inner emotional health or tranquility.

Why carnality generates significant emotional distress is because of its nature. Carnality, or an unspiritual lifestyle, is the deification of the desires of the flesh.

> Consider yourselves to be dead to sin, but alive to God in Christ Jesus. Therefore do not let sin reign in your mortal body that you should obey its lusts, or desires (Romans 6:11-12).

The choice in carnality is to focus our lives around sin with its lusts, or appetites, or focus ourselves around God the Father and our identity in Christ. The striking reality is that God's competition is our own appetites. That is what makes carnality *carnal*, because the word means "fleshly." When a person makes appetite the center of all, it stands to reason that emotional chaos will start invading the life. Appetite says "I want, I want," and the wanting person is always discontent and anxious.

A Life of Misrule

Carnality is a life dominated by misused emotions and appetites. It is a choice for lust rather than God. Strikingly, as we noted, the believer either deifies his appetites or his God. Romans 6:11-12 personifies sin and places it across from the person of God the Father. Sin even has a voice; that voice is the siren call of the appetite. The believer is told not to listen to the call of the appetites; for when a person listens, god has become the person's belly (Philippians 3:19).

Such emotional unhealthiness can be seen in Paul's letter to the Galatians, where he contrasts a life organized around spiritual qualities (5:16) and a life organized around the flesh. After setting the two decisions in front of the believers, he describes the works or habits of the flesh.

> Now the habits or works of the flesh are evident, which are: sexual immorality, dirty-mindedness, and indecency, idolatry, sorcery, hatred, strife, jealousy, outbursts of anger, disputes, dissensions, factions, envying, drunkenness, carousing,

and things like these, of which I told you before just as I have forewarned you that those who are practicing such things shall not inherit the kingdom of God (verses 19-21).

A significant number of the habits of the flesh involve addictive behaviors, as we saw in chapter 2: sexual immorality, impurity, sensuality, carousing, drunkenness, and rageaholism (enmities, strife, outbursts of anger, disputes, dissensions, factions). Others involve very powerful emotions that disintegrate the inner life, such as envy and jealousy. None of those describe anything that is emotionally healthy.

In Ephesians, Paul describes those emotions that invade relationships—emotions that are not submitted to the Spirit of God to change. Notice how powerful they are.

> Stop grieving the Holy Spirit of God, by whom you were sealed for the day of redemption. *Let all bitterness and wrath and anger and clamor and slander be put away from you, along with all malice.* And be kind to one another, tenderhearted, forgiving each other, just as God in Christ also has forgiven you (4:30-32).

The first and last verse describe what the ministry of the Holy Spirit is, which is to make us tenderhearted, forgiving people. The middle verse contains what the opposite is. That verse describes an ocean of emotional turmoil. What if a man went to a psychologist and said, "Doctor, I am angry all the time. I cannot forgive people. Out of the blue I will suddenly break out in a rage of nasty words and actions. Do you think I am emotionally healthy?" Due to training, the therapist will keep a straight face, but probably the first thing he will do is send the person for a prescription of tranquilizers. The second will be to start therapy, and the third will be to send the person also to an anger-management group.

The very essence of a non-existent spiritual life or carnality is emotional pain and turmoil. It is the reign of selfishness over God and life. When a choice is made for the flesh, an abandonment of love, joy, and peace occurs.

THE CHRISTIAN'S FOUNDATIONAL EMOTIONS

True spiritual life is a life overflowing with healthy emotions. The primary emotions we have looked at are love, joy, and peace. Emotions are to the heart what sensation is to the flesh. Sensations tell us when our body is in pain sometimes before our eyes perceive the damage. Every once in a while I have placed my hand on a hot burner, and I have sensed the sensation thankfully before I have seen the damage. The sensation has done a favor for me. Oftentimes emotions tell us the condition of our soul and relationships before our mind often understands it. Anxiety, fear, and envy tell me that my relationship with God is unhealthy. Peace, love, and joy tell me the opposite.

The Bible deals repeatedly with these emotions and other positive ones. In the last portion of this chapter, we're going to take a look at how the Bible promotes these emotions that are so foundational to the Christian life.

Peace

Everyone will say that spirituality is a deep relationship with God and that it is built on prayer. They will also say that true spirituality has to be built on the Bible and the practice of its truths. So let us take a careful look at a biblical passage on prayer that teaches on how to relate to God the Father and how it leads us to the emotion of peace.

> Stop allowing yourself to go on being anxious, but in relation
> to every anxiety by prayer and a request for help after thanks-
> giving, let your specific petitions be known to God, and the
> peace of God, which surpasses every thought, will guard
> your hearts and thoughts in Christ Jesus (Philippians 4:6-7).

Notice that prayer, as I have said in the previous chapter, is not built around a schedule but around a negative emotion, anxiety. Therefore, the whole process of relating to God in this passage is aimed at dealing with the pain of fear. Every anxiety matters to God because we matter to Him. He does not want His children in emotional pain. Peter says this nicely.

> Cast all your anxiety on him because it is a concern to Him
> about you (1 Peter 5:7).

So anxiety is an issue to God—and therefore, it should be an issue to us. Further, this should lead us to start praying to God, to relate to Him. This is another important biblical truth: Our relationship to God determines the state of our emotional life. The emotional life is a by-product of the relationship. If we want to deal with managing the feelings within, we need to seek the Father above.

As we seek the Father above, another adjustment has to take place within us. The requests we make to the Father should be with thanksgiving. We have to decide who is greater, the threat facing us or our God. We have to decide that He is greater by faith. We need to gamble by faith on His ability to deal with threats and His capacity to calm our nerves. The person who does not exercise trust should not expect anything from God due to the emotional and ethical instability within (see James 1:6-8).

Notice that the great Christian virtue of faith is called for to deal with anxiety. As we exercise faith, we then can make specific, concrete requests of Him. If you have just experienced a pay cut and that is making you fearful, you can make a specific request of God the Father in faith and ask Him not only for the money you have lost but also a specific increase of the amount. So what happens in the real world is also connected to the great realities of the spiritual life, such as the Fatherhood of God, prayer, trust, and thanksgiving.

> *What is the proof that effective prayer has been made to the Father? It is the emotional transition from anxiety to peace.*

The end result of this process of prayer is incredibly emotional. The peace of God (the *shalom* we have talked about) which surpasses any process of thought will take up guard around your heart and your thought processes. Paul is saying that the tranquility God provides is so powerful that it will not be disturbed by bad thinking, and it will also be distinct from threatening circumstances. What is the proof that effective prayer has been made to the Father? It is the emotional transition from anxiety to peace.

Joy

The Bible also helps us with another rich emotional component present in the growing spiritual life, and that is joy. In relationship to joy, the same principle will reappear—that a healthy spiritual life is a deeply healthy emotional life. We have looked at Romans 15:13 before; it describes how joy and peace can enter the life.

> Now may the God of hope fill you with all joy and peace in believing, that you may abound in hope by the power of the Holy Spirit.

How is joy different from peace? Peace is a positive sense of well-being but joy is a satisfaction with life and relationships that leaves the heart delighted with God. It is satisfaction and delight in God, life, and others. Notice that joy does not come unbidden; again, it has spiritual conditions connected to it. The Christian has to relate to the Father again, as in Philippians 4, and expect the encouraging work of the Spirit of God. The Christian's responsibility again is to exercise faith. In the midst of this spiritual process, these emotions—joy, peace, and hope—will fill the heart. Let's put it in a slightly different way:

1. Recognize the lack of feeling of joy.

2. Exercising your faith in God's promises is one of the most crucial ways to step into a life of joy. Joy has many aspects to it, but every variety of joy and peace comes through the process of believing by the inherent strength provided by the Spirit of God.

3. This exercise of faith should be done until we are emotionally overflowing.

Notice how the emotional complements the spiritual and makes it real. That is why a healthy spiritual life and a deeply healthy emotional life are the same thing.

Love

The last emotion we will quickly examine is love—the emotion everyone wants to receive and, every once in a while, will want to give away. Love for the Christian is again part of the spiritual process, but as always, it flows out of the relationship with God. First John 4:18-19 expresses that this passionate delight that enters the believer's life starts with Him.

> There is no fear in love; but a mature love casts out fear,
> because fear involves punishment, and the one who fears is
> not matured in love. We love because He first loved us.

For the believer, the experience of having God's passionate delight in their life starts with God the Father. It does not start with us. (Having this experience of divine love and passion to a large extent revolves around what we will be sharing in the next three, crucial chapters. The next chapter will develop how the pictures within us determine the emotions inside of us and the quality of relationships outside of us.)

How do we know that this is an intense emotion that 1 John 4:18-19 is describing? When we study language, noticing the use of opposite words is the most effective way to accurately discover the meaning of a word in context. In the two verses, the opposite to love, or a mature love, is fear and the fear of punishment. No one would say that fear is not an intense emotion, particularly when it is connected to punishment. In the text it is mature love that throws out fear. The positive emotion replaces the negative emotion. The more love matures, the greater the emotional force it will have in our lives. We will have it as we experience God's enjoyment of us—and that is based largely upon having biblically healthy pictures in our life as a foundation for growth.

❧ ❧ ❧

God is emotional, and He has created us with emotions. As we relate to Him in a spiritually healthy way, we also have a healthy emotional life, which we have defined as that kind of emotional life a medical doctor would envy: a happy, peaceful, loving one.

Having healthy emotions also reflects a healthy understanding of God's word. A carpenter's level is used to tell if things are straight or at the proper angle in construction. I have an old one I really like, one that belonged to my father, and this particular level has three bubbles: one for horizontal, one for vertical, and one for 45-degree angles. Peace, love, and joy are like that level. Those emotions tell us if we are constructing our lives around a spiritual relationship with God and caring relationships with people. If those emotions are not there, some pretty unhealthy ones probably are.

In our spiritual construction project, we are now going to spend part 2 working with the powerful tool that is too often overlooked in the evangelical church, as we've seen—and that is pictures of God's view of reality that we can place in our hearts. This tool is not overlooked in the Bible, though. Pictures are the most powerful way of tapping into our emotions. We will see that the pictures the Bible provides for us will open the door to a truly rich, emotionally deep life with God the Father.

PART 2

The Power of
a Picture

5

The Imagination
Is the Key

By THIS POINT IT SHOULD be inescapably clear that evangelicals—who take the Bible and Jesus with great seriousness—have trouble understanding the role and function of the emotions. Emotions are ignored, downplayed, and mismanaged.

Indeed, when we go to certain churches, the best and sometimes only advice we receive is that Christians should ignore emotions and not trust them. That's like telling the pilot of a plane to ignore hurricanes and lightning storms. It's not wise advice. If we manage emotions well, we can soar on the healthy ones and effectively work with the painful ones.

We've already touched several times on the special importance of biblical pictures in managing our emotions. These pictures will bring the peace and joy that God has promised in His Word. But we must apply them to our emotions via our imagination.

The pictures that inhabit our imagination have an immense and controlling effect on our emotions. Any eighth-grade girl can be an illustration of how this works—and any parent of an eighth-grader has seen it. Some boy with pimples glances in the girl's direction once, and her imagination takes over. What is in it now is a picture of this boy trembling with romance at the very thought of her. Her heart and imagination are fixated on the young man.

However, when he glanced at her with empty eyes, he was actually re-enacting a computer game within his head in which he was crushing the life out of Krull the Cruel. He gazed at her for long seconds because his own imagination had him on a different planet fighting for his life. She took that glance and made a romance! Now when she walks by him in the hall, her heart soars with excitement, and she longs to hold his hand. Her desires, emotions, relationships, and perspective are enslaved to what is in her imagination.

The Role of the Imagination

I have a joke I tell that very few people laugh at, but I think it's hilarious. In fact, I consider it one of the funniest jokes I've ever thought up. It's this: *The only thing evangelicals use the imagination for is not to have dirty thoughts.*

It's yet to bring down the house anywhere. Though I think it's funny, I also think that for many evangelicals it cuts too close to home. Unfortunately, an awful lot of Christians spend their lives specializing in what they *don't* do instead of specializing in what they should do. One of the things we should do that will deeply

> *The imagination for the Christian should be our way of stepping into the unlimited resources and love of our Father.*

change our lives is to use God's great gift of imagination positively and powerfully. It is a critical part of the spiritual life.

More than a few Bible believers are nervous about using their imaginations, however. One huge reason for that is how the very word *imagination* is used in our culture. *To imagine* or *imagination* carry with them in English the sense of creating something that does not exist and never will exist. *To imagine* is to deal with what is not real.

The Bible is opposed to this concept. It very powerfully and clearly describes how God's gift of the imagination should be used. When we look at the Old and New Testaments, we see that what we are to do with our imaginations is to picture life the way God really sees it. This is a crucial point to grasp. The imagination for the Christian should be our way of stepping into the unlimited resources and love of our Father. We can recreate God's picture of life within ourselves. *God's intent for the imagination is for us to use it to see the world the way He does!*

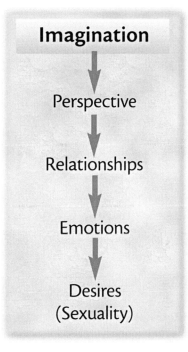

Imagination

Perspective

Relationships

Emotions

Desires
(Sexuality)

God never intended that our emotions and imagination (and, indeed, our sexuality) should be areas of ignorance or nervousness. Instead, the Bible has a clear pattern on how these relate, as shown in our diagram again. The imagination is at the top of how we function in life. We will show in this chapter and the next that the imagination, or the pictures we paint on our hearts, are critical to how we look at life. Those pictures will control our perspective—how we look at life and others. And our imagination and perspective will determine the health of our relationships. From the influence of those three realities—imagination, perspective, and relationships—our emotions will result. Our emotions will be the fruit of what is above them. Then, as we have seen in previous chapters, our desires and appetites will either be inflamed or managed based upon what we do with our emotional states. (We saw all this in the example of the infatuated eighth-grader.)

Religious Suspicion

Sadly, the biblical use of the imagination is sometimes opposed in various circles in the church. I teach at a seminary and often supervise students in ministry projects they have to complete as part of their education. Two students were leading an adult Bible study using our organization's material. Part of that material involved the imagination of the participants. Just as I asked you to do in chapter 1, they were asked to picture themselves at the cross while Jesus was dying. One of the church elders objected to that. He felt that the use of the imagination was unbiblical. He could not quite explain what the problem was, though, except to imply that people were creating graven images in their imaginations!

Some people define life narrowly and seem to forget that it was not Satan who created the world and us. God did. And when

He did so, He pronounced everything He had made as exceedingly good (Genesis 1:31)—including the imagination. Satan did not say within himself, *Now that Adam and Eve have fallen, I will create an imagination within them so they can become* really *rotten.* Contrary to that, evil is the *misuse* of that which was originally created by God for good. Evil cannot create a gnat or rearrange a single atom, but like a parasite it takes over that which was originally good.

Part of the strategy of Satan to nullify the power of the church is to make its members uncomfortable with our own insides so that we do not use the blessing of our emotions and imagination the way God intended. (This is also true of our sexuality, but an in-depth discussion of that will have to wait for another book.) The story that follows is a good illustration of this, and it will also lead us into Jesus' revolutionary teaching about God's real intent for our imagination.

Carrie had been in an unhappy marriage for years. Her husband was a bitter, angry man whose health was declining, and she felt worthless and sad. She attended one of our seminars where she heard she was worth a Son to God, and that she had an Abba Father in heaven. More than that, this Abba Father delighted in her and loved her for the unique person she is. That had a profoundly positive effect on her. She decided she would make it her ministry to love her husband in Christ's stead and to help and serve him as his health declined. She told me that she found a deep and abiding joy in doing that.

A number of others in her church had also benefited from our seminars, so we were invited to do a community outreach there. As we prepared for the seminar, a woman violently objected to the use of the imagination in our material. She had come out of a cult before being a Christian, and she told everyone that our use of the imagination was cult-like and demonic. (She forgot that when she was in the cult she also drove cars, had friends, used money, and breathed with her lungs. She had no problem using these things after her conversion but, interestingly, isolated just the use of the imagination.)

I was asked to meet with the pastors and elders of the church to defend my use of the imagination from the Bible, which I did. They agreed to let the outreach go on. It was obvious, though, that the senior pastor was nervous and appeared to be intimidated. In front of others, the complaining woman also verbally attacked Carrie, who was a loving, white-haired saint in her seventies at the time, and much older than the other woman.

Several years later Carrie asked if she could lead a Bible study using our material. After much deliberation with the pastors, she was turned down and told not to give anyone our books, not to quote me, and not to encourage anyone in the church to study what we say. Throughout these experiences, Carrie was delightful. She prayed for the pastor and her persecutors; she had an excellent sense of humor about it; she just wanted to be helpful to people, share the blessings she had received, and love everyone. (Certainly that kind of behavior will get *anyone* in trouble, won't it?)

The church was one that prided itself on knowing the Bible and doing the right things. Tragically, when they saw a woman profoundly changed by the Spirit of God in front of their eyes, that mattered far less than their own religious prejudices.

Christ's Revolutionary Use
of the Imagination

The church that gave Carrie such a hard time exhibited all the anxieties of the fearful religious. With fear comes suspicion. The church leaders were suspicious of the use of the imagination and of an emphasis on the emotions, and they were not concerned with the management of the inner life.

Religious leaders who are preoccupied with doing everything right and nothing wrong are nothing new. Knowing the right information and doing the right things have always been the goals of the religious person's existence! Religious types have been around for thousands of years. Jesus dealt with them too. The Gospels of Matthew, Mark, and Luke were particularly written to deal with religiosity and its adherents.

Religion Turned Upside Down

One of Jesus' great assaults against religion is the Sermon on the Mount. In that assault, He is going to show us

1. what the emotions are really supposed to tell us

2. what's really important is what's inside, not what's outside

3. what the new world is that we should embrace with our imagination

The practical value for you and me is that Jesus is going to give us a new way of living from the inside out. He is going to break preconceptions that existed in His time and are present in our own. These misconceptions are

1. emotions are insignificant

2. outward activity is more important than the inner life

3. the imagination is simply evil

With Christ, the imagination comes into its own. The Sermon on the Mount is a turbocharger for the human imagination. At the latter part of the sermon, Jesus will use the imagination to transform the heart. To examine how He does that is like viewing the work of Michelangelo, or listening to the music of Bach, or watching the figure skating of Peggy Fleming.

To appreciate the force of the sermon, we have to imagine ourselves in the ancient world. In the second year of Christ's ministry Judea, Galilee, and the regions about were under the control of the Roman Empire. Puppet governors held sway under Roman despotism. Taxes fluctuated from 18 to 30 percent depending on how greedy and how needy Rome felt. The high priesthood in Jerusalem was held by those who were from a completely different family than Aaron's (the family God chose); that family was thoroughly corrupt.

The most admired people in the nation were the Pharisees because they were religious enough not to knuckle under. But they were more than religious enough to put endless rules on serving and worshiping God. What they demanded as standard religious practice was so time-consuming and detailed that only the very well-off could practice Judaism. Christ described the people as being overwhelmed with religious obligations and worn out by religious practice (Matthew 11:29-30). He said that as they stumbled along with both arms filled with their religious burdens, they were set upon by religious and political wolves who threw them down and were chewing on them (Matthew 9:36).

Contrary and Confusing

As religiously polluted, politically oppressed, and spiritually bankrupt as the people were, how could Jesus cut through the confusion, pain, and mistaken teaching?

He simply turned their religious world upside down. The culture assumed that blessings came from sincere effort and a strong will. Godliness, in their thinking, was knowing the right information and doing the right things—much like evangelical culture today. His opening poem turned the world on its head.

> Blessed are the ones who have no more energy, have given up on their own efforts, who are poor in spirit, for theirs is the kingdom of heaven.
> Blessed are the ones who are continually mourning, for they shall be comforted (5:3-4).

Christ's poem is perversely contrary to what the religious expect, and it is concretely confusing: like being hit with a piece of concrete in the center of one's religious assumptions. He said that if you were poor in spirit or lacking religious energy or fanaticism, the kingdom was yours. Those who were rich in spirit, or full of spirit, normally were religiously driven. Even more amazing, if you were continually mourning, you would be comforted (by implication, by God). In other words, the worse off you were emotionally, the better off you were spiritually. He was using their emotional states to tell them something tremendously important: If you felt like giving up and felt lousy continually, you were blessed!

In a nutshell, Jesus was telling the people that the solution to life was not with them but with God. The person who gave up on self-effort was the person God was looking for. If you are one of those who believes you cannot live the Christian life or a truly moral life, Christ is telling you this is spiritually healthy thinking!

Jesus Creates a Crisis

The opening poem praising lack of religious initiative is followed by two snapshots of the disciples as salt and light. Immediately after that, Christ emphasized that the real issues of life are decided deep in the heart. This emphasis on the inner life and the crisis He then creates go on for close to 40 percent of the sermon.

Christ wanted the people to appreciate that the real challenge was in the inner life. He turned His listeners' religious world upside down and dumped them into a bucket of discomfort. He took their collapsing and ineffective religious system and pushed it over a cliff.

The audience He was speaking to was already burdened and loaded down with guilt and a sense of spiritual failure. Feeling deeply unclean, the people flocked to John's baptism and repented at John's message. Wallowing in guilt, they wanted it washed away! Jesus, instead of washing it away, plunged them into a volcano of condemnation. They lived in a deeply legalistic and rule-bound culture, and instead of relieving their pain, Jesus increased it. He shared His expectations: "Whoever then sets aside one of the least of these commandments…shall be called least in the kingdom of heaven" (Matthew 5:19). None of the expectations of the Law would be lowered or ignored.

For many who listened that was not a great surprise, but Jesus then delivered a shock.

> For I say to you, that unless your righteousness goes far beyond that of the scribes and Pharisees, you shall not enter the kingdom of heaven (5:20).

The scribes and Pharisees had a "patented path" to God's kingdom. They were completely confident about their approach. They felt God was in heaven with a special smile just for them. They were the envy of the ordinary Judean and Galilean because they had the rules, the time, and the determination to live the life they told everyone God wanted. No one could do better than the Pharisees. At least that's what they said.

Immediately every stomach in the crowd knotted. If the Pharisees weren't cutting it, not a chance existed that anyone else could. That started the descent into the pain of guilt that Jesus wanted. From the statement about the Pharisees, Jesus proceeded to bludgeon everyone's sense of religious security and well-being. He took 11 common topics the Pharisees taught and the people attempted to practice, topics that reflected their universal beliefs about what a righteous person should do. Christ was going to use the wrecking ball of His righteousness to demolish the flimsy house of religious prejudices and self-serving practices.

The Deeper Issues

To see what Jesus did to the unexpecting people who were listening to Him, let's take a few examples. The common belief was, as it is today, that murder was an act that put somebody beyond God's mercy and was absolutely condemned. All murderers go to hell. Christ took that belief and showed that deeper issues were behind that and needed to be addressed.

> You have heard that the ancients were told, "You shall not commit murder," and "Whoever commits murder shall appear before the court."
> But I say to you that everyone who is angry with his brother shall be guilty before the court; and whoever shall say to his brother, "Raca," shall be guilty before the supreme court; and whoever shall say, "You fool," shall be guilty enough for the burning hell (5:21-22).

Murder, according to Christ, was only a symptom for despising and hating a brother within the heart. The outward act is the fruit of the inward condition, and that condition was enough to send a person to hell! Immediately, into the listeners' minds must have punched the thought, *If that's true, then a lot of us here are destined for hellfire*. Like a fog rolling in, guilt began to take over the hearers' hearts: *We have to be better than the Pharisees, and He's saying we're no better than murderers!*

Another example of Christ taking an outward act and connecting it to an inward condition occurred a few verses later. The Old Testament Law demanded death for adultery. Adultery in some of the villages was still punished by stoning, though within the cities Roman law forbade execution. Christ went directly to the heart condition behind adultery and made no distinction between the act and the desire driving it.

> You have heard that it was said, "Never commit adultery," but I say to you, that everyone who continually looks on a woman to lust for her has committed adultery with her already in his heart (5:27-28).

Guilt exploded through the hearts of the men. Their worlds of fantasy—for some, entire universes of illicit lust—were called what they really were: adultery. (Some may say that sexual fantasy harms no one, but it offends God, corrupts the person, and immeasurably degrades women.) The crowd further thought, *We have to be better than the Pharisees, and He's saying we're on the same level as adulterers and murderers!*

Remember when you first heard or read the Sermon on the Mount, and the anxious thoughts it created? Endless repetitions of its contents and the endless shortcomings of our lives have blunted its knife edge. But for the audience in front of Christ, it struck like a newly sharpened sickle cutting through grass. Everyone listening was succumbing to creeping despair. Insight occurs when we're startled out of prejudices we are barely aware of, and Christ's surgically sharp words cut open hearts and showed the decay.

Each topic Christ addressed—anger and hate, contentions with a brother, lust, stumbling, divorce and marriage, oaths, revenge, dealing with enemies, alms and fasting, prayer, and judgmentalism—was taken back to the condition of the heart that erupted into the acts.

Jesus Points to the Imagination

As the thousands listened, they murmured to one another, "It's impossible!" "We can't ever become what He asks." "We'll have to become new persons." "This is depressing." "I can't stand all the guilt I'm feeling." "I'll have to become somebody else than who I am to do these things!"

Jesus had them where He wanted them: despairing and guilty. Now they were ready for a series of answers. What the crowd's failing really was, was not their guilt or their shame, but their lack of imagination. They could not imagine they could really become what Christ was asking. He challenged them with His comments on being poor in spirit; He struck them with guilt; and now He was going to deliver them through their imagination.

The only force able to place Jesus' listeners into a new world was the imagination.

Neither will, nor memory, nor reason could deliver them. The will cannot dismiss depression, bid guilt be gone, and tell despair to disappear. Will is *driven by* the emotions, but will cannot bid them to *change*. It would be easier for the will to command Mount Everest to move than to tell anxiety and guilt to cease. Nor can memory help at all. All memory can do is record the history of failure—and record the attempts of the heart to avoid seeing the pervasive lust, hatred, and anger inhabiting the soul. And reason can only deduce that what was true in the past will be true in the future. It can only plot the decline into degeneracy, not stop it. It cannot order the approaching tides of the ocean to retreat; nor can it order the heart to become white as snow.

The only force able to place Jesus' listeners into the real world was the imagination. With 16 illustrations He would take them into a new world, with a new picture of their hearts, and with a new Father God. They did not need character, or will, or deep minds, or memories of a history of righteousness. What they needed was a willingness to see reality the way Jesus saw it.

A New Heart Is Needed

Jesus started with the inner life, for that was where the pain of guilt was. He used three pictures for His listeners' imagination: those of a treasure, a lamp, and a master. He first showed them how to recreate the heart.

> Stop laying up for yourselves treasures upon earth, where moth and rust destroy, and where thieves dig through and steal. But lay up for yourselves treasures in heaven, where neither moth nor rust destroys, and where thieves do not dig through or steal; for where your treasure is, there will your heart be also (6:19-21).

The thought of a treasure naturally focuses the attention of the heart, and a treasure easily becomes the most important object of the heart's attention. Jesus shared a way of managing the life of the heart by choosing the ways of heaven as the most important reality of all.

Jesus' presentation of the picture of a treasure to the imagination of His listeners did two things. First, it clearly implied that His critique of the ways of the Pharisees and Judaism was not a final judgment but simply the background for revealing the starting place for spiritual reformation. Second, the picture said there was a way out. The heart could rearrange itself if the person in faith surrendered it to the imagination.

> The lamp of the body is the eye; if therefore your eye is clear, your whole body will be full of light. But if your eye is maliciously evil, your whole body will be full of darkness. If therefore the light that is in you is darkness, how great is the darkness! (6:22-23).

In the Old and the New Testaments, the eye represented perspective, and the body represented all that is contained within. To the listeners who were caught up with the confusion and guilt inside themselves, the image of the lamp communicated to their imagination that the way out was through making sure that their perspective was clear.

The image served a twofold purpose: It moved the listener's focus off the pain within to a new possibility, a new perspective; and second, it gave hope that a new perspective could change the heart and that the whole body—or everything within—would be filled with light.

The final picture was that of having a choice between two masters, and the obvious implication was that a choice had to be made for the good Master, God. Again the image shifted the person's orientation from the pain within to the new image in the imagination, and at the same time it opened the door to the new possibility: We can change if we choose the correct Master.

So the first step in Christ's strategic use of His listener's imagination was to give them a new way of perceiving their inner life. He presented the images of the treasure, the lamp, and the masters as a way out from the guilt and confusion the crowd was feeling. Notice that He did not give a detailed moral pattern as we would find in other parts of the New Testament. Instead, His message of hope was the images for the imagination. First, He filled His hearers with pain, then He drew them into their imaginations to provide hope. Jesus knew that when emotion and the imagination collide, the imagination always wins.

A New World Is Needed

Next Jesus challenged His listeners' perceptions of the world they were living in. His audience felt overwhelmed by the power of Rome, the taxes of the tax-gatherers, the pinch of poverty, and the despotism of their governors. The heartlessness of Pilate the Roman governor was more than matched by the savagery of the reigning Herod. Jesus' listeners inhabited an anxious world.

In the face of those anxieties, He painted a picture within their imaginations of the world as God the Father and He really saw it. "Stop being anxious," He said.

> Look at the birds of the air, that they do not sow, neither do they reap, nor gather into barns, and your heavenly Father feeds them. Are you not worth much more than they?
>
> And which of you by being anxious can add a cubit to the length of his life?
>
> And why are you anxious about clothing? Observe how the lilies of the field grow; they do not toil nor do they spin, yet I say to you that even Solomon in all his glory did not clothe himself like one of these.

But if God so arrays the grass of the field, which is today
and tomorrow is thrown into the furnace, will he not much
more do for you, O men of little faith? (6:26-30).

Placing the pictures of the well-taken-care-of birds and lilies
in His audience's imaginations, He described to them what reality
was really like. God takes care of the lowly animals and plants—
will He not also take care of humans, who are more significant
than the planet itself? Since God feeds the birds and He clothes
the plants, will He not do the same and more for those made in
His image? In fact, people had an added advantage over the birds
and plants—they could plant, harvest, and spin! But even as they
did those things, God still took care of them.

Several years ago I saw a striking picture on the back page of
a counseling brochure. It was a drawing of a man in a prison
cell. He was seated on his bed with his head in his hands, not
moving. But the cell door was wide open, and the chain that had
held his left hand was ripped off the wall and resting on the
floor. Yet the man was not moving. Everything in the picture
said he was free except the slump in his shoulders, the position
of his head in his hands, and the condition of his heart. The
prisoner first had to imagine that he was free to leave. Then he
would *feel* free, and then he would take the first steps toward
freedom.

Jesus was giving pictures of freedom to those imprisoned by
anxiety, guilt, and confusion. He was painting a picture within
their imaginations that would give them the new world they
could enter by faith. The beauty of the imagination is that when
we focus on the pictures, we enter the world of the pictures,
and the emotions of our hearts rise to match the pictures. We
can exist emotionally within that world and feel its security and
care.

But Jesus was not creating a false world, an escape, for them. Instead He was painting a picture for them of the world as it really is. God does take care of humanity whether humanity trusts Him or not. God's care does not depend upon humanity's faith.*

The wonderful message of Christ in the Sermon on the Mount was that God took care of humanity whether that was believed or not. But in order to step out of the prison cell of their emotions, the listeners first had to allow their imaginations to embrace Christ's picture of the world and God's care so as to feel the sensations of being well cared for. Then, the choice was theirs to embrace that new picture of the world by faith.

A New Father Is Needed

Finally, the most important series of pictures Christ used was that of the new Father. Before and during the time of Christ, leading Pharisees argued over whether God should ever be called *Abba*, or "Dad." Their conclusion was that He should not be. Rabbi Jesus of Nazareth was the great exception to that. He called God *Abba*. A major purpose of the Sermon on the Mount was to give the listeners new pictures for their imagination presenting God as a caring, compassionate Father.

> Be asking, and it shall be given to you; be seeking, and you shall find; be knocking, and it shall be opened to you. For everyone who is asking receives, and he who is seeking finds, and to him who is knocking it shall be opened.
>
> Or what man is there among you, when his son shall ask him for a loaf, will give him a stone? Or if he shall ask for a fish, he will not give him a snake, will he?

---

* In verse 30 Christ called His listeners "men of little faith." In the Gospel of Matthew that was a nice way of saying they did not have any faith at all. The phrase "men of little faith" occurred in Matthew 6:30; 8:26; 14:31; 16:8. Each time Christ pointed out the nonexistence of faith.

> If you then, being maliciously evil, know how to give
> good gifts to your children, how much more shall your
> Father who is in heaven give what is good to those who ask
> Him! (7:7-11).

Christ informed His listeners that heaven has a God who, as people are praying and asking, is continually giving. As they are seeking, they are being found by God. He is a God who is continually relating and who is opening the door of heaven to those who are knocking. Jesus then gave the reason: God is a good-hearted Dad who gets a charge out of giving good things to His children. He is not a perverse, dysfunctional parent who enjoys disappointing a child's heart and not meeting that child's needs. In fact, He is better than a good human parent in that He is not tainted by human evil. God the Father aggressively answers prayer and aggressively cares.

In fact, it was one of the major themes of Christ's sermon that God's care comes uninvited.

> I say to you, love your enemies, and pray for those who are
> persecuting you in order that you may be mature sons of
> your Father who is in heaven; for He causes His sun to rise
> on the evil and the good, and sends rain on the righteous
> and the unrighteous (7:44-45).

God the Father cares for humanity whether humanity has any care or concern for Him. God takes care of humanity whether humanity trusts Him or not. God also knows what we need before we pray—so that issue does not have to be the great preoccupation of prayer. Heaven does not need a grocery list from us. Rather, our important duty, as Christ pointed out, is to hallow, or set apart, the Name of the Father in heaven—in other words, to have a clear understanding and picture of the One we are praying to (6:9).

It is important to remember that there were only a few references to God as a Father in the Old Testament. Part of Christ's great mission was to introduce and reveal Him. "No man has seen God at any time; the only begotten Son, who is in the bosom of the Father, he has declared Him" (John 1:18).

Christ is determined to introduce to the hearts—the deepest imagination of men and women—the Person He loves most of all, the Father. It is the Father who is at the center of Christ's pictures concerning the inner life: He is the Treasure the heart should value; He is the Person the lamp of the inner life should shine upon; He is the Master the disciple should choose in the face of the other masters of this world. Why? Because it is only the Father whose care and affection is consistent. Only He is worthy to be at the center of the new picture of the world Jesus wants us to have.

❧ ❧ ❧

Now that we have looked at Jesus' emphasis on the imagination as a route to the Father, the key point I made earlier in this chapter should have a much deeper significance and impact:

- The imagination for the Christian should be our way of stepping into the unlimited resources and love of our Father.

- God's intent for the imagination is for us to use it to see the world the way He does!

That is not the impossible task we might expect. Instead it starts with allowing the pictures God provides to enter our imagination and captivate us, and then permitting the emotions that come from those pictures to rise in our hearts, and finally, acting in faith from that experience.

It follows that the answer for the guilt, confusion, and other painful emotions that so frequently engulf us is to see ourselves, the world, and God the way Jesus looks at them. In the next chapter we will see how crucial a role our human family background plays in keeping us from having God's emotions, not to mention generating negative and destructive ones. We'll also spend more time on working a true picture of the Father into our imagination. If we want to find freedom from the emotional limitations of our family background, we need to connect more and more with the One from whom every true and right idea of *family* ultimately comes.

6

New Pictures for Old Ones

🌿 🌿 🌿

As you have been reading, feelings of guilt and confusion may have surfaced in your heart, just as they did in the hearts of the hearers of Jesus' Sermon on the Mount. This chapter will talk about what the source of those emotions may well be, and how that can be changed through new pictures in your imagination. We'll share how unhealthy family backgrounds often create negative pictures on the inside that deeply influence how we function on the outside. Pictures from "God's family album" may well be the answer to those pictures from the past!

Family life teaches us by thousands of repeated events how to understand life, and how to understand such critical terms and relationships as *father, mother, sibling, love, affection, comfort,* and *trust.* For many, many people the basic pictures they have are a flat contradiction to how the Bible defines those same terms. The result is that when they hear a truth from the Bible, their imagination may paint the picture using pigments from their family background. They may hear the minister say God is a Father—

but the pigments will be a threatening black, a flaming red, and other dark tones.

A dear pastor friend of mine was talking to a woman who had come for counseling. She felt insecure about her salvation and God's love for her. Being wonderfully knowledgeable about the Bible, he went through portion after portion of Scripture describing how God loved her. He got nowhere.

Since the pastor was familiar with my emphasis on pictures, he tried to draw pictures from her life that would illustrate God's love. He asked her if she had any pictures of older men being kind to her. With questions in her eyes, she said no. Then he asked, "Have you had *any* experience of a man being nice to you?" She again said no. (That is tragic, but true, for an amazing number of women.) Stymied, he prayed with her and sent her home.

The woman was lost in thought as she drove home, thinking over what the pastor had shared. Driving slowly through a suburb, she saw on the sidewalk to her right a father and his young daughter. The girl was on a bike with training wheels, and the dad, with an affectionate smile, was walking alongside her with his hand on her back, balancing her. *That's exactly how God the Father is treating you,* was the statement that popped into her mind with force. Quickly she pulled over to the curb, put her arms against the steering wheel, and sobbed. Her emotions felt the love of God and His care for her. The scene on the sidewalk became a picture for her heart because of the thought that was placed in her mind. God gave her a contemporary picture that spoke to her in terms she could understand. The barren desert of her background with its absence of positive pictures was answered by a God-provided one.

The Influence of Our Past

As shown by this story, the pictures from our family background deeply influence how we function as adults. Each of us has a "family picture album," which defines for us the primary relationships in life. If those pictures are unhealthy, it is critically important to change them. This chapter is about identifying those pictures from the past, even the healthy ones, so that you and I can replace old ones with new ones from the pictures God has given us in the Bible. These old, all-but-worn-out ones can be changed by placing over them pictures from God's new family.

The question may naturally arise, Is this something necessary for spiritual growth, or is it just another faddish approach to the walk the Lord wants to have with us? Is it really necessary to picture family backgrounds and God's new family? Part of the answer has to be, obviously, *yes*—because the Bible is filled with word pictures. A mere reading of it will create a continuous picture gallery for the imagination. But I'll answer the question more fully later in this chapter, after we've had a chance to understand the influence of our past more thoroughly.

A couple weeks ago I was speaking at a men's retreat, and I did something I had never done before with a group of men. I divided them up by family background. Frequently in our seminar ministry we will ask groups of couples and sometimes ministerial leadership teams to take a 15-question quiz on their family background—the family they grew up in.* Then, we divide them up into three groups: healthy family background, confused family background, and stressed-out, or dysfunctional, family background. While they are

In many cases the pictures were defining their present reactions to life and God.

---

* I have included this quiz in the appendix, and you will find it very helpful in discovering your own family background.

in their groups, I interview each group as the others listen, and ask basically the same questions of each one.

I was very curious to see how a men's group would respond to this approach. Part of my interest and also concern was that men are supposedly legendary for their lack of interest in what is going on inside themselves and in relationships. So on Saturday morning I took the plunge, gave them the quiz, and divided them up by the results. The approximately 40 men who were there neatly divided up into three nearly equal groups.

After I started the interview process, the men came alive. So much so that on Saturday night, when the men were sharing during communion, a delightful older man in his 70s said, with his mouth almost dropping open with awe, "I have learned more about myself today than I have learned in my whole life."

What we are seeing with this men's group and other groups I have done the same thing with is the power of pictures and the imagination. In the case of these men the pictures were coming out of their family backgrounds, and in many cases the pictures were defining their present reactions to life and God.

Instinctive Pictures of the Father

The Bible says that God is a Father. The key picture of the Christian life deals with this truth. Ask the three different groups to describe how their father functioned at home, and most likely we will get three different kinds of answers. For Family Group One (healthy), the dad was a kind, compassionate man who was very involved with the lives of the family members. Ask Family Group Two (confused), and the dad was distant, removed, and often unreliable. For Group Three (stressed-out, or dysfunctional), they may have actually hated their fathers because they were abusive. Or the mother may have been very abusive, and the dad did not intervene to protect the child.

What will at first sound odd is to say that those basic pictures will have more impact on a believer's life than the information in the Bible about God the Father. That is because the first picture is intuitive and in the subconscious—and the biblical picture oftentimes is just data.

I have taken a number of different language courses, and what I have been told repeatedly is that, for a speaker of a foreign language, words in their native language will always have a far greater force than words in a language learned later. For example, one German teacher told me that saying the Lord's Prayer—or as she called it, the "Our Father"—had a completely different impact when she said it in German than when she said it in English in an American church. What is true of a person's native language is completely true of our "native pictures." Unless the pictures are changed forcefully, the old ones will always trump the biblical ones.

Each of the three family groups has the same basic information from the Bible, but the answers to simple questions are usually strikingly different, particularly from Groups One and Three.

- 🦋 When I ask Family Group One if they have a sense that God the Father likes and love them, they will calmly and casually nod their heads yes and affirm it aloud.

- 🦋 When I ask Family Group Two the same question, they will hem and haw and usually say, "I think so." Then I repeat the question, underscoring the word *feel:* "Do you *feel* God likes and loves you?" Their eyebrows will furrow and their faces will look confused (hence the name for Family Group Two: the "confused" family background), and they will sort of answer yes.

❧ Then Family Group Three, with faces taut, will give a decisive set of no's. One person might say, "God's not supposed to like anybody, but I believe He is obligated to love us." When I ask, "Do you know the Bible teaches that God loves you?" these people will answer, "Of course"—but in the same breath they will say they certainly do not *feel* loved.

The reason for the distinctions is that each is drawing from a different set of instinctive pictures for the word *Father*. Why are these distinctions within the groups so powerful? And to repeat the question from this book's preface, Why is it that the truth—good, solid, biblical truth—that these believers have heard hundreds of times has not changed them? Why is the Bible ineffective in their lives?

It is the crucial difference between *information* and *integration:*

❧ With *information,* the conscious mind has simply placed data in the memory.

❧ With *integration,* the conscious mind has taken a picture formed in the imagination and placed it in the subconscious, where it will affect emotions.

Let's see how this works in regard to three key issues in family life: trust, affection, and openness.

Trust Within the Family Backgrounds

When I divide a group, I always start with those whose scores have placed them in the healthy family-background group. First, I ask whether they have any problem trusting people or trusting God. "No, not at all," is the typical response. Going back to the group at the men's retreat, as I talked with them, one or two volunteered that, when they became adults, that trusting attitude created problems. People sometimes took advantage of them. One said sadly that his trusting naiveté set him up for a troubled marriage because he did not realize how much family background affected adult functioning. He had trusted that his wife came from a healthy background too. Such was not the case. After a good number of years of marriage, they are still sorting things out. As we talked, he looked like a man who had just missed his airplane flight.

Because this was a men's group, some unusual things started immediately. Often men show affection by kidding and mocking one another. Comments that might reduce a woman to tears might actually mean "I like you" in "men-speak." The men in the third group started making fun-loving but sarcastic comments to the first group, such as "I don't believe people like you exist," "You're obviously self-deceived," or "Now I know why you're weird!"

Then I went on to the second group. Their responses were not as uniform as the first group's. Some could trust, others said it was difficult to trust. One said, "I'm always waiting for the other shoe to fall. Sooner or later something goes wrong." That is a typical Family Group Two comment.

Then, I got to the third group, which is almost always is the most colorful and vocal of the three. Often as not they have come out of bizarre family backgrounds, so they carry with them a streak of the different! When I asked them if they had problems trusting people, some of them responded like I was asking a stupid question. "Of course I do," one of the men said. "I'm always waiting to get burned." Then I asked the group if they had problems trusting God. Nearly everyone nodded their head. Their reactions were directly opposite to the first group. (I sometimes refer to group number three as the "opposite world." Shortly I will explain that.)

Affection Within the Family Backgrounds

As I have said, the growing-up years and the pictures from that background determine how the Bible is heard. After asking questions of the groups about trust, the next area I address is what the family did with affection. With the first group at the retreat, I asked, "Did your parents express affection and show they liked you?" Inevitably, the healthy family group, with relaxed smiles, would say, yes—their parents showed or expressed affection. Then I asked, "As you got older, were you able to share emotionally significant things with your parents? For example, when you were a teenager were you able to share with your parents?" Most of the people in group one said they were able to. Exceptions existed, of course.

When I got to group two, the men tended to say no, they did not share the emotionally important things they were going through. I asked why. The men I asked could not put their finger on it. As I asked, I noticed they were looking at each other with question marks in their eyes. I asked, "Was it that somehow or other your parents communicated they really did not want to hear private stuff?" Looking puzzled, the group said that might be the case. As a group, they appeared confused (hence the name); they could not quite explain what had been going on during those teenage years.

A Picture of Confusion

Once I divided up a team of students and staff of Campus Crusaders who were doing a summer evangelism project. Most of the staff were scattered in groups two and three. I called on a woman staffer in group two and asked her, "Did you feel loved as you were growing up?'

"Yes," she said with a pretty smile. "I felt my dad was my best friend. He and I would do things together. Sometimes we would go horseback riding together."

"When you were a teenager, could you tell him things that were emotionally significant or painful?"

"Oh, I couldn't do that," she replied, looking at me as if wondering why would I ask such a dumb question.

"You mean you felt loved and liked, but you couldn't tell him what was going on in your heart?"

She responded in a very straightforward way, "I knew he didn't want to hear about the struggles I was having, so I didn't share."

"But how could you say he loved you if he didn't want to know what was going on in your life?" She did not respond. I continued, "How can you love someone without wanting to know what's going on in their heart?"

Everyone in groups one and three had knowing smiles spread across their faces as they understood that a contradiction—a big one—was going on. One or two listeners rolled their eyes. This intelligent young woman, however, did not see it.

Afterward I talked to her about our conversation. She still did not understand that she appeared to be living in a contradiction. She shared with me more about herself, telling me that one of her sisters had turned out to be a major disappointment to her dad, and sadly, this sister had passed away. The father refused to go to her funeral. I asked if her dad loved that sister, and the young woman said he did. What it appeared to be boiling down to is that the dad did have affection for his children, but he did not know what to do with the inevitable failures and disappointments that children create.

The young Campus Crusade staff person had figured that out, and so she kept her dad in the dark. At no time did the dad and daughter sit down and agree that was the way they were going to relate. The other sister did not join the system of cover-up and therefore ended up excluded from the life of the family. But since that was the family system—be affectionate but keep dad in the dark—that practice became so completely normal that the young woman could stand in front of a large group of people and describe it without seeing any of the inherent contradictions. Everyone else could, though!

Openness in the Family Backgrounds

Let's go back to our men's retreat and the next group, group three. I asked them if they had shared what was emotionally important to them with their parents in their teen years. I was met with a lot of "Are you kidding?!" responses. They of course did not share. Then I asked them what they thought of this observation: "Is it not true that the way you work is that the more emotionally important it is, the less likely you will tell anyone? That 'anyone' also includes the person you are now married to." Looking like they had just been in the back of a car when the brakes were slammed on hard, they immediately agreed. One said, "That's the way it has to be."

A stunning picture brought this home to me in my own life. After Carol and I were married, we adopted two children. Because we didn't want to repeat how we were raised, we made a point of talking to our children every day about how they were doing and how they were feeling. (Not once did my father ever ask me, that I can remember, how I was doing emotionally—or at all. I wanted my children not to have that experience.) As a result, our kids learned the ability to accurately describe their emotions and learned how to comfortably talk about them.

When our children were in their late teens, I was reading a book about families and parenting. I do not remember the title or the author, but I was impressed with what he said about the role of fathers. Fathers cannot solve every problem their children have, he said, but they can sympathize with what their children are going through and can be with them through those problems. As I was reading I was picturing my relationship with my son, and I felt that was what I was trying to do with him.

Suddenly a very powerful comment leapt into my mind: *That means you are a better father to your son than God is to you!* It hit with such force that I thought, *Deep down that must be what I believe.*

What I think happened is that the Holy Spirit saw what I was reading and also saw the picture in my mind of how I was pursuing a relationship with my son, and then decided it was a strategic time to show me what I really believed on the subconscious level.

A Picture Communicates Truth

As I reflected on my prayer life, I realized I did share with God the Father what I was going through but didn't share with Him my deepest emotions. That is because I am from Family Group Three and was practicing the "inverse rule": The more emotionally significant something was to me, the less inclined I would be to share it, even with God.

What the Holy Spirit did with me was what Jesus did in the Sermon on the Mount, as we saw in the previous chapter. Jesus asked the men in His audience, "If your son asked you for bread you would not give him a stone, and if he asked you for a fish you would not give him a snake, would you? Since you, being evil, know how to give good gifts to your children, will not your Father give good gifts to you if you ask him?" (Matthew 7:9-11, my paraphrase). Jesus used that word picture to communicate to His hearers the good heart of God the Father. The Holy Spirit used the picture of my treatment of my son, the comments in the book I was reading, and the thought He placed in my mind to do the same for me.

My prayer life immediately changed, and I started sharing those emotionally significant things with God. I noticed I felt less lonely. Again and again, the irony for me is that I can read the Bible in Greek, Hebrew, German, and French, but the words could not pierce through the fog of my family background until a picture was connected to them. For both me and the woman who had never been treated well by men, God had to take a picture from our lives to communicate to us.

The Crucial Issue of Affection

I believe God the Holy Spirit uses a mix of pictures from our lives and the Bible to reach and deeply change our emotional life. Let's take a look at our three groups again to see how a biblical picture can deeply change them. How these backgrounds influence their understanding of love will be what we look at. All family life revolves around love—whether it is absent or present.

In Healthy and Confused Backgrounds

When I ask the first group whether they felt loved or liked as they were growing up, as we have seen they nod their heads and give an emphatic yes. With the second group, as we have learned to expect, things get confusing. The reason things get confusing with that group is that they often have experienced genuine love and affection, but always in confusing ways. "When you were growing up, did you feel loved and liked?" I will ask. The answer of course is yes. Then I will ask, "But did you also have a sense that you had to *earn* the love and affection?" The answer again will be yes. Often as not somebody from the confused family group will volunteer, "If I did not do what my mother wanted, she wouldn't smile at me for a week and hardly talk to me while she talked up a storm with everybody else in the family. Then, when I did what she wanted, it would be all hugs and kisses."

What I believe is the most common characteristic of the confused family is that love and affection is first granted as a gift, but over time it has to be earned by parent-pleasing performance. Discipline such as spankings or time-outs would exist in the home, but the additional element was added of withholding love and affection for failure and granting it with obedience. Those from healthy family backgrounds normally said they felt loved whether they were performing well or not.

After telling group two that the "yo-yo of affection" was the characteristic of that family type—and also one of the major reasons for confusion—I always share with them the great picture of the cross we saw in chapter 1.

> God commends His own love toward us, in that, while we continually were yet sinners, Christ died for us (Romans 5:8).

I point out that God separates our wretched character from His love for our person, and the cross is the great illustration of that truth. As Christ is dying for our sins, God is recommending His *agape* love. His wondrous love values the person more than it is affronted by the sin. When we were non-Christians, sinking under our malicious hate for God and others, our lack of religious respect, our moral weakness, and our sinning, God saw us. The

Father was in love with the person who was wandering about in the personal fog of wrongdoing.

The confused family group has to deeply meditate on that picture. They need to walk around the cross in their imagination, and then look above it and see God the Father smiling at them. Then they need to be repeatedly saying to themselves, *At my worst moment Christ is dying for me—so that I understand that God loves me whether I have character or not.*

In the Dysfunctional Background

Family Group Three is entirely different from the other two. Rarely have they experienced pure, undeserved affection. When asked to describe how they were raised, they will describe harsh punishment. "The only time a man touched me while I was growing up was to hit me," said one young man. Numerous divorces occurred; vicious words and family fights are common in the descriptions the group gives.

This group can surely give you the dictionary definition of love and affection, but something deeper than confusion is present. The problem of the Wycliffe Bible Translators is occurring. How do you describe a camel, sand, and snow to someone who is wearing a loincloth in the jungles of Brazil? With difficulty. How do you have a discussion of unearned affection—the gift of liking—to those who may well have never experienced any? Or more tragically, who never experienced any growing up and now cannot spot it or respond to it as an adult? With probably greater difficulty.

A white-haired retired gentleman I was having breakfast with said with a smile on his face, "In the last years, I have made it a point to tell my children and my grandchildren I love them. I know it's important, and no one told me that as I was growing up.

But I still don't have any feeling behind the words." This man always smiled as he talked, but he admitted the smile was "practiced amiability." The amiable smile was less than skin-deep, and it was really a defensive wall against pain.

What I have discovered with group three is that I have to help them out, like helping a blind person cross a street or a lame person to walk. They need to notice not only *that* emotions are absent, but also *why* they are. So I explain to them that with their group, love is *blind loyalty*. The emotional component is not there. That's often the best the group can do. Tragically, that is often how they understand God's affection for them: God the Father is blindly loyal to them, but otherwise He feels nothing.

"That's amazing—I can understand that," is often the comment from them. For some people, these moments are an intense period of personal revelation. At the men's retreat, two of the men in group three looked shocked. White-faced and pained, they were stunned deep within themselves to realize they had grown up on emotional empty.

Changing the Dysfunctional View of Affection

If you are not from group three, you may never understand. Sadly, if you don't, you may never appreciate the Niagara Falls of cleansing that the gospel can bring. I deeply appreciate what these people go through.

When I was growing up, in order to survive I had to shut down my emotions and go on blind loyalty. Unfortunately, the longer emotions are shut down, the harder they are to find, and rarely

> *In the "opposite world," love means blind loyalty, and trust means a lower level of suspicion.*

will they surface on their own. When I met Carol in college, I fell deeply in love with her. It was romance at its best. She was lovely, bright, and charming, with a smile that filled up the day!

After I asked her to marry me, all my deep feelings for her disappeared. *Nothing* was in their place. I was shocked, confused, fearful, and told no one. (As I've mentioned, that is how group three functions. If it is emotionally important, keep it to yourself.) That lack of feeling lasted for the next 18 years of our marriage. I never talked about it because I was clueless as to what was going on. But I followed instinct. I became blindly loyal. I knew how to do that. Any time I attempted to sort out what was going on, I would feel like I'd walked into an electric fence of shame. I would be knocked back 20 feet, so to speak, and would give up the effort.

For people in group three, two things have to happen. They must understand they are living in the "opposite world." Almost all, if not all, of the important words dealing with relationship have been contaminated. The pictures they have to draw on are deeply painful. In the "opposite world," *love* means *blind loyalty,* and *trust* means *a lower level of suspicion.* They must recognize they have a "Sermon on the Mount" crisis on their hands, explosively rebel against where they are, and pursue inhabiting a different world.

Secondly, they must be very careful to find pictures that match the truths of what they say they believe. Otherwise, the grossly distorted ones from their growing-up years will define their new world of Christianity. Without a second thought, they will respond to God's affectionate love for them with blind loyalty; and to God's trusting them with His purposes and plans, they will respond with a lower level of suspicion.

New Pictures of God's Love

For group three, simple pictures of what love is have to be deeply meditated upon. Paul did that with the Thessalonian believers. He wrote to them that they were his beloved—the recipients of *agape* love.

> Because we long to be with you, we thought it was a good idea to share not only the gospel of God but also our own souls because you had become our deeply loved ones (1 Thessalonians 2:8).

He also said he had deep longing for them and affection, telling them he did not flatter them nor do a cover-up or put on a "cloak" to hide greed (verse 5). Then he used two snapshots to describe his depth of affections. First, he said that they were like the emotions of a nursing mother.

> We acted as gently as children among you, even like a nursing mother nurtures her own children (verse 7).

Modern researchers have likened nursing mothers or new mothers to drug addicts who can't get enough of the drug—the drug being the baby. They have an ocean of affection for the child. That, Paul said, was the way he felt, and this was because he had *agape* love for them. Then he used the snapshot of a good dad raising his children.

> ...just as each of you knows how we were encouraging and tenderly urging and affirming even as a father would his own children (verse 11).

Paul used two of the basic positive pictures of human existence to represent how *agape* love appears: a nursing mother who has endless affection, and a father who has an emotional and personal investment in his children. That is what *agape* love looks like. It is deeply emotional.

Christians in the third group need to begin to deeply meditate upon what God means when He says He loves us. It means He has the tender feelings of a nursing mother for us and the tenderness of a good, healthy dad for us. I strongly suggest to those from Family Group Three that when they pray, they first picture how God views them. They should picture the Father smiling at them affectionately. Then they should picture an affectionate nursing mother, and then a delighted dad with his children. Finally, they should thank God the Father for His feelings for them. Each and every time they pray, they should do this—until they feel His divine affection. If it takes ten minutes or ten months, they should work at it until the Spirit of God fills their hearts with the Father's affection.

Family Strengths and Weaknesses

Over the years as I worked with these groups, I have pointed out the strengths and weaknesses of each. Each time I do this, the groups themselves actually will "picture," or illustrate, what I say.

1. Family Group One (healthy family background)

   - *Strength.* The words, pictures, and emotions they have match each other. They can become great helps to others from the other family groups because they innately understand health.

   - *Weakness.* They often approach the problems of life with platitudes. They have good emotions, but they lack real compassion for the abused of this world because that world is so foreign to them. As a result, they may lack courage and confidence in the gospel to change lives. Often they will act like Christianity is just the moral wing of the Republican Party.

2. Family Group Two (confused family background)

- *Strength.* They do have positive emotions to build on, and they can feel deeply the pain of life. They can weep with those who weep and rejoice with those who rejoice.

- *Weakness.* They instinctively want to *earn* love; and the emotions they have, they will mismanage. Often they will mistake *knowing biblical information* for *integrating biblical truth.*

3. Family Group Three (dysfunctional family background)

- *Strength.* They have an understanding of the deep pain of life, and often as not, they are not afraid of life. Also they often become the most daring and creative Christian leaders.

- *Weakness.* In the face of their suspicion, they need to consciously choose to walk by faith daily. If they become Christian leaders, they may institutionalize their dysfunctions. They have to consciously work against that.

The Characteristics Become Obvious

These strengths and weaknesses make themselves very obvious. I can distinctly remember an experience I had when I divided up a very large group of seminary students. We had a lot of time available, so I spent it having each person give a snapshot of their growing-up years. As the third group was describing how they were raised, one student said he lived in the backseat of a car. That was his home. Others described sexual abuse and physical abuse.

During those sad stories, I walked back to where the first group, those from a healthy family, were seated. Several of them were crying. "Why are you crying?" I asked.

One student responded, "Because it is sad." Another said, "I feel terrible. I have been attending school with them for years, and I didn't know their stories. This is heartbreaking."

Group one has the capacity to weep, but they do not have the capacity to imagine tragedy. They have to make a pointed effort to enter the world of others, or they have to have that world brought into their lives the way it was done in the class— so they can realize how privileged they are. Sadly, they reflect much of the evangelical church, which acts as if all of life is fun. It is not.

Those from a confused family background also have the capacity to weep. Oftentimes with that group, tragedy has visited the family. When each has an opportunity to describe family background, often as not the story ends with tears. Mothers who have died from cancer, or fathers who moved about in the military, are often mentioned.

The major difference occurs with the third group. When they describe tragedy, they do so without tears. As recounted, it has all the pathos of a weather report. Incest victims describe their sorrowful experience like they were reading from a newspaper.

I then ask the members of the Third Family Group how they feel about the tears and sorrow among those who come from a healthy background. The responses are usually of three different types. "It makes me irritated," one person will say. "They could cry forever and never understand." Or a woman will say the sympathy makes her uncomfortable, and she doesn't know what to do with it. A third will say he doesn't feel a thing. Characteristically with this group, they do not know what to do with sympathy. Receiving compassion takes life experience and training. They have not had it, so they do not know what to do with it.

The Only Way to Embrace the New Truths of the Present

We have shared two sets of pictures: one set from various kinds of family backgrounds, and another set from the Bible and others that are in harmony with the Bible. Now we can more fully answer the question as to whether this understanding is necessary for spiritual growth or is just another faddish approach. Is it really necessary to picture family backgrounds and God's new family?

I firmly believe that we have to get in touch with pictures from the past to practice the Christian life in the present. It is utterly necessary—or Christianity will be an exercise in platitudes and abstractions. The gospel's sharp iron edge will be reduced to the mushiness of oatmeal.

Paul the apostle, in writing to the Ephesians, told them they had to come to terms with their pasts to embrace the new truths of the present.

> You were not discipled by Christ in this way, if indeed you have heard Him and have been taught in Him, just as truth is in Jesus, that, regarding your former conduct, *you take off the old identity*, which is being corrupted by lying lusts, and that you *be continually renewed in the spirit of your mind*, and *put on the new identity*, which in harmony with God has been created in righteousness and holiness of the truth (Ephesians 4:20-24).

Paul told them they had been taught to take off the old identity so as to put on the new. What is the *old identity?* Christians who are inclined to theology might say that is our participation in Adam; it is our union in the fall of humanity and everything that went with it. If we could try that explanation on the Ephesians, probably a great look of confusion would come over their faces. That would be an incomprehensible answer. It would probably be more sensible to tell them to take off the feathers of the great stork than to tell them that.

Laying Aside Evil Practices and Unhealthy Pictures

What did Paul mean by *old identity?* He himself helps us with the answer by using similar phraseology in Colossians (Colossians and Ephesians are quite similar in content). There he wrote, "Stop lying to one another, since you laid aside the old identity with its *evil practices*" (Colossians 3:9). Obviously he meant all the evil practices that are connected with our old past, our old identity outside of Christ.

In other words, these are all the concrete evil practices that came from family backgrounds, cultural backgrounds, and daily life outside of Christ. Another way of putting it is, take off those unhealthy practices that are inherent in Family Groups Two and Three especially—and the lacks of Family Group One, such as a lack of compassion. Paul was not talking theoretically but *practically.*

The only effective way I have found that a person can start to meaningfully lay aside these evil practices is to compare and contrast the three family groups. The comparison and contrast will bring out the unhealthy practice of trying to earn love, the practice of substituting a lower level of suspicion for true faith, the practice of mouthing words of affection as opposed to having deep feelings for one another, the practice of mouthing platitudes instead of being clothed with compassion, and all the other unhealthy realities that belong to each family group.

As we compare and contrast, not only will concrete practices come to mind, but also the unhealthy pictures from the past that need to be changed. What Paul was talking about in Colossians 3:9 was not just lying, but also the emotional confusion, false pictures, and ineffective communication from the past. Because of all of that, words have to be joined to the pictures they come with and then be compared to the biblical words and the pictures they come with—so that we are really, actually, putting on the new identity.

Everything Renewed

This putting on also demands a total change of thought within. After Paul said to put off the old identity like clothing—that is, make sure the old way of looking at yourself and relating to God and others was put away—he then said to "*be continually renewed in the spirit of your mind*" (4:23). The mind was to be made completely new; everything was to change. As we identify what we are wearing from the past, we are to put that away and then embrace a completely new way of thinking, so as to put on the new identity in Christ with the new practices.

The importance of comparing and contrasting the family backgrounds—and also cultural backgrounds—is that it cuts through the confusion that accompanies family life.

The temptation to be avoided is the embracing of platitudes and a mere rearrangement of practices. For example, a person like myself from the Third Family Group might learn that a Christian is supposed to be compassionate and caring. (Tragically, with that family group, emotions have been so shut down that the person might think it would be easier to practice weightlessness than to have a rich emotional life.) So the person may thoughtlessly and quickly substitute a "practiced amiability" that has been developed over the years instead of godly compassion and spiritual joy. The smile we may be wearing is as authentic as if it had been painted on with water colors.

That is why Paul was demanding a complete renewal in the thought life and in the human spirit. When Paul made that demand, he was breathing in the spirit of the Sermon on the Mount. There, as we saw in the previous chapter, Christ presented pictures of a new world, a new Father, and a new inner life. Everything had to become new.

Paul also had a new set of pictures for the believer to embrace so that a thoroughly new way of thinking, feeling, and relating could be embraced. The importance of comparing and contrasting the family backgrounds—and also cultural backgrounds—is that it cuts through the confusion that accompanies family life. All the same words are used in the three family backgrounds as well as God's new family, but the meanings are often somewhat different to completely different.

✿ ✿ ✿

The challenge is a significant one for us, but we do have an effective process. As you can see again in the diagram we've been using, the crucial starting point is the imagination.

As the imagination is engaged and changed, the perspective is altered. Then, how the individual relates to God, family members, friends, and others also is changed.

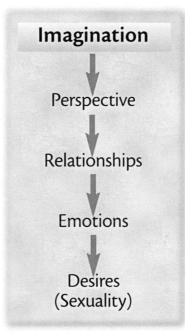

In the next chapter we will show how each Person of the Trinity has a particular set of pictures He wants us to place within our hearts—our imaginations. As each picture is embraced, deep and powerful changes will occur inside us.

7

God the Father's Favorite Pictures

"How many of you carry a wallet?" Hands went up all around the auditorium. I pointed to a young man with a backward baseball cap on his head and asked, "What do you carry in your wallet?"

Taking his gum out of his mouth, he responded, "Money, credit cards, and pictures."

"Who are the pictures of?"

"My wife and my children."

"You have pictures of your wife and children," I said. "And why do you have them?"

His eyebrows went up in surprise. "Because I love them."

"Well, that is very nice—but why do you carry their pictures? Do you ever look at them?"

The young man said, "I look at the pictures because when I look at the people in the pictures, it brings me joy."

I told him thank you for the information, and I went on to ask the entire group, "How many of you have video cameras?"

A number of hands went up. I asked a well-dressed, white-haired woman near the front, "Why do you have a video camera?"

"I like to take pictures of my grandchildren," she said.

"Do you take pictures of the children just standing around?" I asked.

Laughing, she responded, "No, I take pictures of special events the kids are involved in."

"What kind of events?"

"Birthday parties, soccer games, school graduations, anything I consider important."

I asked why she did that.

"It brings me joy to look at the videos later."

"And why do they bring you joy?"

"Because the pictures are of people I love."

Wallets and video cameras are great, but God does one better. God the Father does not carry a wallet, nor has He invested in a video camera. He has done something far more marvelous to remind Himself of the Person He loves and the central events of that Person's life. He has a wonderful set of pictures of Jesus—and we are it.

The Ultimate Picture

When someone becomes a Christian, the Holy Spirit joins that individual to Jesus Christ so they are in union with Him. The Spirit also joins the Christian to the central events of Christ's life: His suffering, death, resurrection, and ascension to heaven. The result is that we have become a picture of the person and work of Christ to the Father. He does not use a wallet photo to remind Him of His Son, nor does He use a video to preserve His memory of His Son's great work on the cross. He uses us! If we realize that emotionally and picture ourselves the way the Father sees us, our lives will be changed, and our emotions will be managed. That is the ultimate picture to imagine and live within. Living within that picture, everything changes.

The Father has made us walking, talking reminders of His Son. We have to picture ourselves that way. The great Person of the Redeemer, and the great pictures of His Redemption, are ours!

The Source of the Father's Joy

In our home we don't have empty picture frames on the walls, nor do we have those posed photos of strangers that come with frames from Wal-Mart. But as you go from room to room, you'll see we have photos of our two children. In our bedroom we have framed drawings of our children done when they were young. Not all the available space in the home has a picture of our children, but a lot does.

God the Father, however, has turned every available Christian—that's every one of us—into a picture frame for His Son as well as a video screen for His Son. The reason that the Father has made us reminders of His Son is that the Father's great joy is His Son!

At the very beginning of the ministry of the Messiah, the Christ, God the Father gave His opinion of His Son. (This was at John's baptism of Jesus.)

> ...and listen, a voice out of the heavens, saying, "This is My Son, My Beloved One, in whom I am well pleased" (Matthew 3:17).

He described His Son as being His Beloved, or the object of His *agape* love; and also the One who has brought Him pleasure, or with whom He was well-pleased. God the Father and the Son have been in an eternity-long love relationship. All through that relationship, the Father has found in the Son an infinite source of delight.

This love is expressed two ways in the Greek of the New Testament. One term is *agape,* which means to have a passionate delight in someone or romantic love for a person; and the other is *phileo,* which means to have affectionate feelings for a relative or a dear friend. John the Gospel writer described the Father's feelings for the Son:

> The Father passionately delights *[agape]* in the Son, and has given all things into His hand (John 3:35).

Then, Jesus, speaking of the Father's feelings and actions toward Him, said that the Father has *phileo,* or the affection a person has for a close relative:

> The Father really likes *[phileo]* the Son and shows Him all which He Himself is doing. And greater works than these He shall show to Him in order that you may be astonished (John 5:20).

The Father and the Son have a wonderfully delightful love relationship. The Father infinitely values His Son. Everything that is of value in Christianity flows out of that friendship! All the values of biblical Christianity flow out of their relationship. That shared great love gives the work on the cross its infinite value.

Jesus Is at the Center

The sacrifice of an American soldier's life in war may have sentimental value for an American citizen who does not know the soldier. But everything changes when that soldier is a well-loved son or daughter. Suddenly the sacrifice of the soldier takes on an intense, great value. That is the kind of value God places on the work of His Son on the cross: intense, infinite worth. This reality is forcefully illustrated by the scene John saw in heaven, where he found himself before the throne:

> I saw in the middle of the throne (with the four living crea-
> tures) and in the middle of the elders a Lamb standing, as
> if He had just been slain, having seven horns and seven eyes,
> which are the seven Spirits of God, sent out into all the
> earth (Revelation 5:6).

In the middle of the throne of God, a Lamb stood as if He had just been slain. The very center of heaven, the Heart of God, is fixed on the just-dying Son. This riveting picture tells us what is central to the heart of the Father. Eternally in the eyes of God the Father, Jesus is always before Him as the innocent, defenseless Lamb who has just been slain. Heaven is transfixed by the very moment of the Lamb's death.

Once I was teaching in a church and I mentioned that, to a parent who has lost a child, the death of that child is a timeless event. It is not just in the past; the picture of the dying child is carried in the present and will be carried into the future by the grieving parents. Two days later I received a note from one of the pastors of the church. He had experienced the death of a baby daughter 15 years before, and in two paragraphs he described in detail his baby's dying, the hospital room, his emotions, and his wife's. To him it is an ever-present event.

The Son of God's dying is the ever-present event of heaven. The book of Revelation is our tour of the heart of heaven. The word *Lamb* occurs 29 times in the book of Revelation—the most common title for Jesus in it. That title tells us what matters to God the Father—and that is the work of His Son on the Cross.

Union with Christ—Because of God's Love

Christ's Person and Christ's work are the eternal center to God the Father. For the Trinity that is the great reality. No other greater treasure exists. No other picture would have greater worth, and no other video would have more significance. God has joined us to that picture and placed us in that video.

His motivation for placing us there is love for us. The same love that fuels the Father's passionate delight and family feeling for His Son drives the reality of our union with Christ. Never forget that it is the Father's love for us that places us in Christ; He did not place us in Christ to create a reason to love us. Rather, because He loves us, He placed us in Christ. As I have previously emphasized, it is critically important to remember that God's love fell upon us before we were saved or placed into Christ:

> God, being rich in mercy, because of His great passionate love with which He passionately loved us, even when we were corpses in our trespasses, made us alive together with Christ (by grace you have been permanently saved), and raised us up with Him, and seated us with Him in the upper heavens in Christ Jesus, in order that in the coming ages He might show the surpassing wealth of His grace in kindness toward us in Christ Jesus (Ephesians 2:4-7).

God's love is driving His desire to have us in union with the Son. This union with the Son has eternal ramifications. The Father's love for us and our union with Christ result in God being kind to us throughout all the rest of eternity. What we have done does not determine the Father's love. What He has done for us displays His love toward us.

God's New Picture of Us

The Father pictures us joined to the Son. When we became Christians, we were joined to Christ. In Galatians it is described as though we have put Christ on like clothing:

> All of you are mature sons of God through faith in Christ Jesus. For as many of you as were immersed into Christ have been clothed in Christ. There is neither Jew nor Greek, there is neither slave nor free man, there is neither male nor female; for you are all one person in Christ Jesus (Galatians 3:26-28).

Because of this, we are mature sons of God through faith in Christ Jesus. Probably when you read the phrase "mature son" in the verses of my translation, a twinge of tension went through your soul. You thought, *That is certainly not me.* Calm down and let Paul's point have its way. Paul is taking customs from the culture of his time to explain to his readers that God is treating us the way mature sons were treated in the Greco–Roman world. It is important to recognize the significance of being a mature son for the culture of that time.

When our daughter, Adrianne, was in high school, she went to a conference called "Women in the Sciences." She came back aggravated and as mad as a hornet. She said they had told her she could be anything she wanted to be and she was as good as any man. Well, it had never occurred to her she was not! She was red hot because they had implied she thought she wasn't. She said she was angry because we had taught her not to be conscious of her gender but to be conscious of all she could do—and that was nearly anything.

Unfortunately, 2000 years ago, women were third-class citizens everywhere. So when Paul said to women and men that they were all mature sons in Christ Jesus, the women of the ancient world breathed a huge sigh of relief. Finally, someone would treat them as well as the sons in the family, and that someone was God Himself.*

---

* Today, saying someone is a son of God leads to the question, "What's wrong with being a *daughter* of God?" But in Paul's time, being treated as a son was great for women. We'll see more about this in the next chapter.

Earlier in the chapter Paul also contrasted God's treatment of the Jews under the Law and His treatment of Christians with the sending of Christ. With the former, God gave them endless rules so they wouldn't make mistakes and so they would be protected from themselves and others. With us, He did not hand us a set of rules but instead placed us in Christ. We have *put on* Christ. The words for "put on" actually mean to be clothed with Christ.

This union with Christ so identifies us that differences disappear. Religious differences, being Jew or Greek, do not matter because we are clothed in Christ. Social conditions, being slave or free, do not matter because we have a status greater than either. Gender differences do not matter, because being identified with Christ carries with it a greater significance than the innateness of male or female.

God's New Picture of His Son

This identification not only pertains to how God the Father sees us—it also defines how the Father sees the Son. When the Father looks at the Son in heaven, seated on His throne next to Him, He sees us.

> Even when we were corpses in our trespasses, (He) made us alive together with Christ (by grace you have been permanently saved), and raised us up with Him, and seated us with Him in the upper heaven in Christ Jesus (Ephesians 2:5-6).

Notice that the union with Christ is twofold: He is joined to us, and we are joined to Him. When I was 17 and still a new Christian, I read a wonderful book that told me for the first time about my union with Christ. After I was done reading it, though, I was actually sad. The impression I received from the book was that being in Christ meant that I disappeared. Christ was all in all, I was completely covered up, and God did not see me anymore. I received the impression that God wanted no part of me, because He had to totally hide me in Christ.

Only years later did I realize that God does not want to cover us up with divine whitewash, but instead wants to put us and His Son in union. He loves us as a person, and He loves His own Son—and out of affection for us both, He has placed us in union. We are as identified with Christ as He is identified with us!

God the Father's Favorite Video

We have also said that we are made into a video of the central works of Christ's life. The family history of Christ is made our family history. Paul described this in Romans 6.

> Do you not know instinctively that all of us who have been immersed into Christ Jesus have been immersed *into His death?* Therefore we have been *buried with Him* through immersion into death, in order that as *Christ was raised* from among the corpses through the glory of the Father, so *we too might walk* in a new kind of life. For if we have become *united with (Him) in the likeness of His death,* certainly we shall be also (in the likeness) *of His resurrection,* knowing this instinctively, that *our old self was crucified with (Him)* (Romans 6:3-6).

Paul asked those he was writing to, Did they not know by their life's experience that they had been baptized, or immersed, into the central events of Christ's life? When we see the word *baptize* in the New Testament, it is used of being plunged, dipped, or sunk into, or surrounded by, something, or someone, or some experience. In the context of Romans 6, it is used of being plunged into the events of Christ's life. The other term being used for our union with the events of Christ's life is "united." *United* literally means to be "planted together" or "grafted." When a graft occurs, eventually we cannot tell where the original tree or plant and the graft begin or end. They have become one—united.

In summary, Paul tells us we have been joined to

- 🌿 Christ's crucifixion
- 🌿 Christ's death
- 🌿 Christ's burial
- 🌿 Christ's resurrection

The central events of Christ's life are counted to be our own.

This is critically important to get hold of. When God the Father looks at His Son He sees not only us, He also sees us participating in the great events of Christ's life. He sees us being crucified with Him and suffering with Him. He sees us dying with Him and being buried with Him. Best of all, He sees us being raised from the dead with Him. This makes the difference between hiding in the shadows and drinking shame, or living in the light and love of God's presence. We need to see ourselves the way the Father sees us.

Believe God's Point of View!

Carol and I have been married for more than three decades. We are quite happy, and there are a number of reasons why. A major reason is that we believe the other person's perspective. For example, I like to give Bible conferences and teach at retreats. For the first few years of our marriage Carol would come along and never complain. Then she finally sat me down and said,

"David, I do not like to go to these conferences because I am an introvert, and they just wear me out." I could not believe it; she had cheerfully gone along and been a great help. She added, "You talk to everyone in sight; if I could talk to only one person all weekend it would be just fine. But everyone wants to talk to me! If we are gone for two days, it takes me three days to recover."

> *"When My Son died, you died with Him— and I am happy to completely accept you just as I accept My Son."*

I had assumed that since I was an extrovert I must be marrying an extrovert. I had never put it together that I had never seen Carol speak to more than one or two people at a time. Even though it seemed very strange to me and I was amazed, I took her word for it. That is how marriages survive: People have to believe the unbelievable things their spouses say.

It is the same way with God. To have a healthy relationship with Him, we have to believe the way He sees things. When He looks at a Christian, He instantly sees that Christian joined to Christ and participating in His suffering, death, burial, and resurrection. If we walked up to God the Father in heaven and asked Him what the three most important things He knows about us are, He would say, "You suffered with My Son; you died with My Son; you were raised with My Son. Those are the most important events of your life, and the most important things I know about you!"

A woman might respond to God the Father, "The most emotionally devastating and shameful experiences I have gone through were my two divorces. Surely those have to be the most important thing You know about me!"

God the Father answers, "My Son died for the two divorces as well as the affair you haven't mentioned. When My Son died, you died with Him—and I am happy to completely accept you just as I accept My Son."

Another woman might say, "I worked as a prostitute and had two abortions, and now I'm convinced abortion is murder. Those have to be the most important things You know about me."

"The most important events I know about you are that you suffered, died, and were raised with My Son. That's what matters to Me, and that should be what matters most to you," says God.

"I've cheated on my taxes and stolen money from work for years—I'm sure that's what matters most to God," a man says. The answer from God is always the same—He sees us joined to His Son.

"I have struggled with homosexuality and have been involved sexually with men. That has to be the most important thing God knows about me!" a very uncomfortable young man says. Again, the most important thing that God knows about this Christian is that he has died with, been buried with, and been raised with God's own Son.

Adopted as the Firstborn

In some ways I can understand what God is doing with His Son and our adoption into His family because our two children are adopted. They both came into our home when they were two days old. What they received from us was not only our name, but also all of our memories, relationships, friends, and family. Our history became their history. The most important events of my life, such as my marriage to Carol, naturally became the most important events of their life.

When we signed the adoption papers for our son, Andrew, a pleasant woman who was clerk of the court of the City of San Francisco took Carol, the baby, and me to the judge's chambers. The judge said this adoption would be the happiest thing he did all day. With the smiling clerk looking on, he read us every word of the two-page adoption decree. He got to the words, "Andrew Brian Howard Eckman will be treated with all the rights and privileges of a biologically born child of Carol and David Eckman. To not do so is to defraud Andrew and invite the penalty of the law," and as he read them, I was filled with deep emotion. That was exactly what I wanted to do, and hearing it expressed brought tears to my eyes.

That is what the Father has done for us. He is treating us like the firstborn Son, and He has shared with us the family history. He has done for us out of love what the law of man demanded Carol and I should do for our children out of obligation!

God's Delight with His Decision

Is God just being nice about this? Is He being like a co-dependent rescuer on a bad day, desperately trying to make everyone happy? Not at all! It is striking that the same language used of God the Father's love for and good pleasure in His Son is also used for us. What that means is that God is deriving great pleasure from our union with Christ.

> Blessed (be) the God and Father of our Lord Jesus Christ, the One having blessed us with every spiritual blessing in the heavenlies in Christ, just as He chose us in Him before the establishment of the earth, that we should be holy and blameless before Him. *In passionate delight* He previously destined us to adoption as adult sons through Jesus Christ

to Himself, according to the *good pleasure* of His *settled desire* (Ephesians 1:3-5).

God's good pleasure, or His being well-pleased, has also embraced us. He has in passionate love adopted us as mature sons and daughters in union with His Son. In verse 3 above, we participate in all of this "in Christ." The two great emotions God shared when He spoke of His Son at the baptism of John—"This is my passionately loved Son in whom I am well-pleased"—are the two emotions He shares with us.

The phrase "good pleasure of His settled desire" found in verse 5 above has two elements involved. The word for *good pleasure* refers to the pleasure one feels as he or she thinks about something deeply satisfying. The words "settled desire" refer to the settled desires of the heart. Combined together, as they are in this verse in Ephesians, they say that when God thinks about joining us to Christ, He feels good pleasure, and doing so satisfies a settled desire of His heart.

So, in a nutshell, how does God feel about you and me being joined to His Son? He feels great. It brings Him great satisfaction. He looks at our sin as being joined to the blood of Christ, and He looks at us as being joined to His Son. Our responsibility is to live within that pleasure and use God's picture of us as the basic definition of our life before Him.

Most Christians would just like to be tolerated by God; to be delighted in by the Father is unimaginable to many of us. Most Christians would like to get to the point of feeling accepted by God once a week; yet Ephesians tells us we have every imaginable spiritual blessing in heaven in Christ. If we want the blessing of being secure, we have that blessing in heaven, where it matters. If we want the blessing of being loved and forgiven, we have that blessing in heaven, where it matters.

God's Command About the New Pictures

Before we go on, let's go back quickly to God the Father's favorite video—Christ's "family history." We are now part of that family history and are joined to each of its events:

- ❧ Christ's crucifixion
- ❧ Christ's death
- ❧ Christ's burial
- ❧ Christ's resurrection

These pictures of Christ are the Father's new set of pictures for us. He wants this new set to replace the old pictures in our family album, and so in Romans 6:11 we are commanded to do two things:

> Even as Christ is alive to the Father so you are ordered to assume yourselves to be dead to sin, but continually alive to God in Christ Jesus (Romans 6:11).

First, we are to assume that this new set of pictures gives us full permission to relate personally to God the Father. And second, we are to use this new set of pictures to deal with sin within—the unbridled power of emotions and appetites.

Romans 6:11 is not a suggestion from God—it is a command. It is telling us to take for granted that we are in Christ and joined to the Son's suffering, death, and resurrection. We can see how important this command is if we think about two things:

1. *This is the first command in the book of Romans.* Paul has spent six chapters and ten verses telling his readers that God has delivered us from sin and joined us to the Son in a new creation of humanity. Almost certainly this is

also the *most important* command in the book of Romans because everything flows out of it. Everything in the spiritual life has to flow from the assumption that we are in Christ. And this command is in complete harmony with Christ's picture of the vine and the branches, when He says that apart from Him, we can do nothing (John 15:1-4).

2. *Romans 6:11 may be the most important command in the New Testament.* And if that is true, then it has to be the most important command in the Bible. True, one could argue that loving God with all our heart, mind, and soul is the most important command. But practically speaking, how can we begin to love God if we do not live out of our identity in Christ!

To sum up, God is not giving a suggestion to us about living our lives out of Christ—He is giving an absolute order. Nor is God giving us a nice picture to warm our hearts. He is giving an absolute command to live according to how He pictures us. He pictures us in Christ. We are not the sum total of all the failures in our lives, nor the sum total of our last dozen sins—we are the sum total of what God has done for us in Christ.

Picturing Ourselves Dead to Sin

Paul also says that not only we are to use this picture to relate to God, we are also to use it to assume we are not alive to sin. Sin inside us has its own set of pictures it wants us to live our lives around. Sin has its own set of video clips it wants us to live our lives through. Because of the culture, the church, and poor preaching, many Christians base their lives on video clips of spiritual failure. Video clips of pornography, sexual immorality, or masturbation may flood the mind of a Christian man and make him ashamed of relating to God or praying. A Christian woman may have her own set of video clips from sin that involve sexual immorality or unethical behavior. Or she may have pictures of someone shaming her or humiliating her, and those have become the defining pictures of her life.

God the Father does not suggest to us that we *try* a new set of pictures to define ourselves in relation to Him. He flatly *orders* us. Really, we have no choice. Being joined to the suffering, death, and resurrection of Christ is the set He wants us to use.

Many times people have failed so often in the Christian life that they almost have a sense that they "owe" it to sin and themselves not to picture themselves differently before God. In a strange kind of way, we think that, if we abandon ourselves to a completely new way of viewing ourselves before God, we will be breaking some obligation we have to our past and its failures.

Sin walks us into a huge warehouse filled with video clips of us and says, "This is your life. We have thousands of clips of your failures. Many of them are so embarrassing that you wouldn't want to show them to your children. That is all you are, and we have the record of it. So you might as well surrender to sin within, because you can't be better than this. You are these clips—and nothing else."

Well, from God the Father's perspective, Jesus has burned the warehouse! Instead of going into the warehouse, playing some clips, and surrendering to sin, we are ordered in Romans 6 to assume that we are just alive from the dead. A person who is alive from the dead has no obligation to the past, and is simply supposed to enjoy the new world he or she has been resurrected into:

> Stop presenting the members of your body to sin as instruments of unrighteousness; but present yourselves to God as

those alive from the dead, and your members (as) instruments
of righteousness to God (Romans 6:13).

Not only are we to assume that we are continually alive to
God in our union with Christ, we are also ordered to stay around
His Presence. In the phrase "present yourself to God," the word
present literally means "to stand around." It means standing
around someone, awaiting that person's orders. Because of Christ
and our union with Him, we need not apologize for our existence. Instead we can share our lives with God, owing nothing to
our past and its shame. What God sees every time He glances at
us is our suffering with Christ, our burial with Christ, and our resurrection with Christ. Having this foundation, we can be brutally
transparent with God the Father about what is going on in our
lives.

❧ ❧ ❧

No Greater Heritage

The picture and video God has of us should become instinctive. Part of the great heritage of being raised in a healthy family
is to feast emotionally from the memories, the pictures, of that
family. When I am around people who are emotionally healthy,
invariably they are bringing into their hearts pictures their parents
gave to them of how much they were treasured. People who are
emotionally unhealthy are drawing on massive reserves of sad pictures and tragic videos. It is as if they have been trapped in the
horror-movie section of the video store and cannot escape.

Several years ago I read a summary of research on people who
had survived and prospered even though they had come from

heartbreaking backgrounds. The research said that the common factor with each person was that some adult had liked them and invested in their lives. That person might have been a coach, or a teacher, or a relative. But it could have been almost anyone—though that "anyone" had to have been a person who looked upon them with love.

The most remarkable story was told by a very successful, mature woman who had come out of an abusive childhood. The person in her life was Captain Kangaroo. In the hell that was her home, she would turn the TV on and watch the Captain look out at her affectionately. She believed him when he smiled and said, "Boys and girls, you are special." She saw herself in his eyes, and she survived and prospered. Starvation for affection and the insatiable desire for a smile in the girl's heart made the words of the Captain life-changing.

If the words of a Captain Kangaroo can change a heart, how much more can the smile of God! The God of the Bible has a delighted smile for His children. When He looks upon us, He sees us joined to His Son, and when He looks at His Son, He sees Him joined to us. With every glance He sees us participating in His Son's suffering, death, burial, and resurrection. You are special to Him. Build your life around His glance, His perspective, His smile, His pictures of you and His Son!

PART 3

Grasping the Love of the Father, the Son, and the Holy Spirit

8

You're a
Grown-Up Now

ℰℰ ℰℰ ℰℰ

I OFTEN ASK CHRISTIANS WHAT the three most emotionally significant events in their lives are, whether positive or negative. Sometimes the responses are delightful; sometimes depressing. One man said all the emotionally significant events all occurred on the same day. On the same day, he graduated from college, he got his acceptance from medical school, and his girlfriend agreed to marry him. A woman said that one, a negative one, was in college when she recognized she had grown up in an abusive home; then another, also negative, was when she realized she did not like herself. Then the last one, a happy one, was when she had met her husband. Her husband was next to her, and she put her head on his shoulder and wept.

Invariably I will ask these people, "Do you have a right to have that perspective on those events?" Looking puzzled, sooner or later they will say, "Yes, we have a right to our feelings and perspective."

I then ask them, "Does God have a right to a different list of events in your life that are emotionally significant to Him?" Invariably they also agree that God has a right to His own list.

What are the three most emotionally significant events in your life?

1.

2.

3.

What is God the Father's list of the most emotionally significant events of your life from His perspective?

1. You suffered with Christ.

2. You died and were buried with Christ.

3. You were raised with Christ.

I repeat this point from the last chapter to emphasize that God has a perfect right to see us as He wants to. As we have learned, we can build our lives around old pictures from the past that will cripple us and leave us afraid of God and ashamed of ourselves, or we can build our lives around the pictures of love that God has of us.

> *God the Father wants the same kind of relationship with us that He has with Jesus!*

Thus, if we are joined with Christ, if we are crucified and raised with Christ, does it not then follow that we should *live* like Christ? Let's start with a picture of how we are *not* to live. At our church every Sunday a young man is brought in in a wheelchair. It's obvious his mind is childlike and he is not what he physically appears. His parents love him greatly and desperately desire to have an adult relationship with him, but though his body is grown up, his mind is not. Similarly, every once in a while near our home I will watch a group of adults with Down Syndrome being taken on a walk with their helpers. These people smile and laugh and look very much like adults, but their minds are not adult.

God has not placed us in Christ so we can repeat either of these tragedies. Rather, God has made us walking, talking pictures of His Son and the central experiences of His Son's life so that we might have the same quality of relationship that Jesus has with the Father. God the Father wants the same kind of relationship with us that He has with Jesus!

Sons and Daughters Like Jesus

In the previous chapter we touched briefly on Paul the apostle's description of us as mature sons of God. This is a crucial part of grasping our standing and participation in God's own family. Just like Jesus, we are not dependent children. The Father has entrusted us with His full resources. As we picture to ourselves how He has trusted us, our emotions will be changed and help us to trust Him.

In Galatians 3, Paul begins to flesh this out:

> Before faith came, we were kept under guard under the law, being locked up in a cell to the faith which was later to be revealed. Therefore the Law has become our child-guide to Christ, that we may be justified by faith. But now that faith has come, we are no longer under a child-guide. For you are all mature sons of God through faith in Christ Jesus (verses 23-26).

Paul described the Jewish experience under the Law as being like protective custody. The Law functioned as a guard—probably a very nice guard—who locked the jail door so the Israelites could not go out and the bad people could not get in.

Then, Paul changed the image of the jailer to the friendlier picture of a tutor, a word that I've rendered more literally as *child-guide*. Often on vases from ancient Greece and Rome pictures of social life were painted. One set of vases has a scene of a child-guide walking a young boy down a street. The guide's job was to make sure the youth got to the teacher's home safely. As the vase is rotated the next scene is the teacher instructing the student while the guide is seated in back waiting for the class to be over. Then, the last scene is the guide taking the child back to its home.

In the ancient world, the guide could give a child simple instructions and go over lessons. But the teacher did the teaching, and the guide did the guiding to the teacher's home. Since the faith has come, Paul wrote, we are no longer under a child-guide, for all of us are mature sons in Christ Jesus. In the context of Galatians 3, the teacher was Christ, the child was the Israelite, and the guide was the Law. The Law's final purpose was to bring the child to Christ and leave him there. It was faith that made the Christian an adult son.

No Longer Children

In Galatians 4 Paul developed the contrast even more so that we could fully understand we are to function as adults and not kids. He took some social institutions from the ancient Greek world to explain what kind of relationship God has created with us.

> Now I say, as long as the heir is an impulsive child, he does not differ at all from a slave although he is owner of everything, but he is under guardians and managers until the date set by the father. So also we ourselves, while we were

impulsive children, were held in permanent bondage under the elemental things of the world (Galatians 4:1-3).

The Jews were like a male child of a rich and powerful man. When the child was young, the father treated him according to the customs of the times—like a slave, even though later the child would become the master of everything. The child was also under managers and guardians. (The father must have been powerful to have so many servants looking out for the interests of the child.)

Paul wrote that was also the state we were all in: We were under the elementary principles of how that age operated. But things profoundly changed with the coming of the Christ.

> But when the fullness of the time came, God sent forth His mature Son, born of a woman, born under the Law, in order that He might redeem those who were under the Law, that we might receive the adoption as mature sons (verses 4-5).

In other words, the Son was sent so that we might be adopted.

Mature Sonship

Here is a critical difference between the ancient world and the modern world. In the ancient world, they rarely adopted babies, but instead they adopted adults. If someone wanted a baby, the supply was endless. Families were large, and babies were sometimes burdensome. So extra babies were sometimes exposed, or put out to die. If a baby was wanted, the question asked would be, "How many?"

Instead, *adults* were adopted. When a childless couple was getting so old that any possibility of child-bearing was gone, if well-off, they would legally adopt a young man whom they loved and trusted to take over the family business and handle the family wealth. This was so the couple would be taken care of in their old age. In fact, the word *adoption* in Greek literally meant "to place an adult son."

Remember the book and movie *Ben Hur*? After Judah Ben Hur rescued the Roman general from killing himself, the general adopted him in the stead of a son who had died. At the party where the general was introducing his new son, a parchment was on the table, a signet ring was on Ben Hur's hand, and sandals were on his feet. The parchment was the legal adoption paper for an adult. The signet ring was the family seal that could be used to buy and sell, and run the family business. The sandals could be worn only by a free person. (According to the law, a slave always had to go barefoot.)

We can easily tell from Galatians 4 that Paul was emphasizing our adult sonship. He contrasted the impulsive child with the strong young man who would accept the responsibilities of adulthood at the time set by his father. Though treated like a slave when he was young, he knew that he was destined to run the family business and rule the slaves as a despot. When he entered adulthood, no longer would he allow himself to be treated as a child or a slave.

The mature son would be insulted if the child-guide of his younger years would come up and say, "I need to guide you around town to keep you safe and protect you from impulsive decisions." Or if one of his father's managers came and said, "I need to make decisions for you still." "I have passed my twenty-first year which was set by my father," the son would say firmly, "and I can make my own decisions. My father trusts me, and so should you. In fact, I order you to!" If one of the slaves said, "You can't give me orders because you were bossed around like us for years," the mature young man could order the slave to be beaten if he wanted.

All of us Christians, both males and females, have received the adoption as full-grown sons. We are viewed as trusted adults who can participate in the family business, make decisions, and have a significant role.

Mature and Responsible

When Paul said we were sons, I suspect a number of us intuitively thought he must be thinking of babies—newborn offspring of God. That is a safe perspective to take, but it is not the right one. If Paul was thinking of merely babies, then no moral expectation can be placed upon us. But if he was thinking of us as mature daughters and sons of God, then we have the responsibility of seeing ourselves the way God the Father sees us. For as the picture of ourselves is in our hearts, so shall our lives be.

When an aged couple in the ancient world did adopt, they were not interested in someone who was irresponsible. Nor were they interested in someone who had to check a rulebook in his back pocket to see what the right thing to do was. They wanted a young man with character and principles, somebody who would instinctively do the right thing.

What God has done for us is to place us in a picture with Christ, and now He wants us to live in harmony with that picture. Instead of a slave relationship or an overprotected child's relationship, we are to have a principled, adult relationship with God. A *principled* relationship is not a simple black-and-white, rulebook relationship. Instead, principled people live life out of noble principles—noble dispositions—in the heart. They live life out of love, peace, joy, and above all, gratitude. Their character is instinctively honest, not merely conveniently honest.

A Relationship of Familiarity

Also, a principled relationship is based on one more key characteristic:

> Because you are mature sons, God has sent forth the Spirit of His Son into our hearts, continually shouting, "Abba! Father!" Therefore you are no longer a slave, but a mature son; and if a mature son, then an heir through God (Galatians 4:7).

Notice how odd this verse would sound if we put the word *baby* in for *son:* "Therefore you are no longer a slave, but a baby, and if a baby, then an heir through God." It just does not sound right, of course. The important thing is the contrast of the downtrodden slave with the freedom and dignity of a son!

God has not only given us the position of adults, He has also sent His Spirit into our hearts shouting, "Abba! Father!" What is the message God wants us to get?

If you called over to Lebanon, and a little Lebanese boy answered who spoke both Lebanese and English (not at all impossible), and you asked him to call his father, you would hear him shouting, *"Abba, Abba,"* in the background—or "Daddy, Daddy."

Abba means *daddy* in Aramaic. The Spirit of God has a message for us: We have a Dad in heaven. The word *father* implies the need for respect. The word *dad* implies affection and familiarity. At the worst moments in His life, Jesus called upon His Abba Father (Mark 14:26). In the stress of the Garden of Gethsemane, Jesus said, "Dad!"

Functioning in Freedom, Affection, and Maturity

God wants one more thing in His relation with us—affection. Since He has an adult, principled, affectionate relationship with His Son, He wants the same with us.

It is no honor to heaven to have Christ capture a group of slaves of sin and turn them into a bunch of religious slaves. His goal is to not only liberate us from the domain of sin and the power of the devil, but to liberate us to function as mature sons of God. Giving us the freedom to be sons was part of the purpose of Christ's coming. Sometimes that was not understood by His Jewish disciples:

> Jesus therefore was saying to those Jews who had consistently believed Him, "If you yourselves remain in My word, you are truly disciples of Mine; and you shall personally know the truth, and the truth shall free you."
>
> They answered Him, "We are Abraham's offspring, and have not once been enslaved to anyone; how is it that You are saying, 'Free ones you shall become'?"
>
> "The slave does not remain in the house permanently; the son does remain permanently," Jesus answered them. "Truly, truly, I say to you, everyone who continually commits sin is the slave of sin. If therefore the Son shall make you free, you shall be free indeed" (John 8:31-36).

Christ spoke of three realities: We would be delivered from sin, we would be free indeed, and we would be permanent sons in the family. The goal was not to produce slaves who would have to be watched and ordered about all the time. Christ's goal was to create brothers and sisters for Himself who, belonging to the same family, lived their lives out of affection and principle.

I was at a wedding for an older friend of mine. He had a number of grown children at the event. During the reception two of his sons sang in honor of the newlyweds. As they sang they looked straight at their father with affectionate smiles, and he looked back into their eyes. All through the song, the sons and the dad had eyes of affection glued on each other. What it illustrated was an adult, principled, affectionate relationship between grown sons and their father. No longer could the grown sons merely obey childish rules. Their lives and their relationship with their father were sustained by the music of affection and character.

Invited into the Family

The adoption we have received is for the purpose of living life in the same mature way Jesus lived His life. In a sense, Jesus and God the Father are standing with their arms around each other, and they turn to you and ask you to stand between them and with their arms over your shoulders. If you accept the invitation, that means you are going to participate in the same quality of friendship and love relationship Jesus has with the Father.

Many believers naively think that when they became Christians, God gave them a more healthy, sane, and wholesome lifestyle. That's true, but still poverty-stricken in thinking. Something far greater has happened. We have been invited into the life of the Trinity through the work of Christ. The Father, the Son, and the Holy Spirit do not check a rulebook or contracts as they relate to each other. Instead they relate out of the affection and principled love binding them together. Since the Holy Spirit is also in our lives, He can help us to become the principled, affectionate daughters and sons that God wants.

In John 17, as Jesus talked to the Father before He went to the cross, He went over what He had accomplished and what He wanted to happen. He had told the disciples about the Father so that the love the Father has for Him might be experienced among those who have trusted in Him. As this occurs, Christ will live in them. The family life of the Trinity is what we are to experience and live out.

> I have made You known to them, and will continue to make
> You known in order that the passionate love you have for

Me may be in them and that I Myself may be in them
(John 17:26).

God the Father and God the Son live in joy, love, and trust.
Those qualities are the very atoms and air of heaven. Our lives,
relationships, and walk with God are to be based on those characteristics. We are to abide in them.

Even as the Father has passionately loved me, I also have
passionately loved you: remain in my passionate love (John
15:9).

A slave thinks about not being beaten and about not missing
a rule. He lives out of fear and envies the status of the family
members of his master. A child lives out of impulses and has to
be protected from himself. A healthy adult sustains relationships
through affection and lives out of principles. "Abiding in God's
love" means not reducing Christianity into a slave mentality and
a fear relationship, but responding to the love and affection that
is being poured into our lives.

The unity of the Father and Son in their trust and love is
being shared with us so that we might participate in such a life of
harmony and unity. Our privilege is to be loved the way the
Father loves the Son.

I in them, and You in Me, that they may be perfectly complete in unity, that the world may personally recognize that
You sent Me, *and You passionately love them, even as You passionately love Me* (John 17:23).

God has no favorites: All of us are His favorites. Nor should
there be spoiled offspring. The goal of the Trinity is to have us
experience the love they experience, and to exhibit the character
of Christ. That is eternal life.

Characteristics of God's New Family

How does this new family identity compare to the other three family types? It shares some similarities with the healthy family and very little with the other two. With the dysfunctional, or stressed, family background, we find that negative pictures from the past deeply affect how people relate, view themselves, and the world. Instead of those negative pictures, our new identity in Christ gives us a positive view of ourselves and an overwhelmingly wonderful family history.

A young woman who lived on the streets of San Francisco buying and selling drugs became a Christian and left that life behind. She was interviewed by one of the major papers in the city, and they asked her how she could leave her past behind. She answered, "I am not the sum total of my past. I am the sum total of who God tells me I am." The responsibility of the person who is in that Third Family Group is to exercise real faith in how God sees us and values us.

In the Second Family Group, or the confused family background, the two great confusing realities are that those family members do not know what to do with love or with emotions. Because their emotions are confused, they cannot live out of principle. Instead, life is lived like people in a rowboat on a stormy lake. Wherever their emotions push them, they go. And typically for the Second Group, love is earned. In absolute contrast, the cross of Christ completely separates love from character. With God the Father, His love can only be accepted or rejected because it is not earned.

Healthy members of God's family compassionately view those outside and have a sense of love for them.

The individuals from Family Group One have experienced love freely given; they can somewhat manage their emotions. Comfort can be given and received. But sometimes healthy families fall very short. People in healthy homes often do not use their great gifts in an outward-directed way for the benefit of other people. As one young man from a healthy home said, "My dad loves us, comforts us, and acts like a coach for our lives. But he always is telling us to not trust anyone outside our own family."

The instincts of God's family are entirely different. Healthy members of God's family compassionately view those outside and have a sense of love for them. It is not a love that those outside the family have earned. Rather, such compassion and love is given as a gift. In chapter 5 we shared what the characteristics of the first three family groups are and summarized them in a chart. Here is the summary for God's new family:

Family Group Four (God the Father's family)

- *Strength.* They have a sense of the affection and trust that make up the life of the Trinity. Because of the sense of being deeply loved and secure, they can notice the needs of others. Eagerly they throw themselves into the family business of rescuing and helping others. They find great joy in their relationship to the Father of the family; they are very proud of the Person and work of the Son; they can instinctively respond to the promptings of the Spirit of God.

- *Weakness.* The characteristics of the other three family groups often interfere with the privileges and affection that is theirs. They have a tendency to reduce life to rules instead of the joy and compassion coming from relationships.

Whatever the family album is that you and I have received from our parents and relatives, we have to put the new pictures over the old. For the picture of a father, we have to superimpose the picture of our Abba Father. For the family history photos, we have to cover them with the suffering, death, burial, and resurrection of Christ. As the old family photos picture things that have become instincts in our lives, we have to choose to live within the new set of pictures so that they too can become powerful instincts in our lives. As we do we will experience the emotions of God's new family—and the greatest emotion is love.

We're Trusted Family Members

Every parent probably would like to have a family business for the children to participate in, and when they get older, to inherit. We have talked about how adult son and daughter placement worked in the ancient world for a childless couple. That naturally leads to the question, What does God want us to do with our placement as adults?

He wants us to respond to the trust He has placed upon us. He wants us to respond aggressively to being placed in Christ and being given a mature adult relationship with Him. Most Christians appear surprised when they discover that God is sharing significant family responsibilities with us. But He is trusting us and relying on us!

After I became a Christian at the age of 17, I was quite surprised when I read the "Great Commission" in Matthew 28. I thought, *How could God entrust such a huge responsibility to slugs like us?* But I needed to remember several things. What He was asking for, He was going to empower us to do, and He was going to place His Son in charge of the universe to help us to do what He wanted. Most importantly, He was going to teach us trust by exemplifying trust. Instead of communicating a lack of confidence to us, God the Father chose to share His Son's mission with us. He made us partners in the family business!

Jesus did the same thing with us. The Son has entrusted His mission to us.

> Jesus said to them again, "Peace to all of you, even as the Father has sent me, so I am sending you" (John 20:21).

Jesus trusts us to be His representatives. In His absence we are His physical presence in the world. His character, His ability, and His gifts have been poured into our lives so we can represent Him on a massive scale. As He breathed on the disciples and gave them the Holy Spirit, He has done the same for us (John 20:22). He endowed us with the power to carry out His plan and simply said, in effect, "I'll turn over my whole mission to you. I'm leaving. You can do it!"

The Son trusts us as representatives, and the Father trusts us as adults. In addition, the Holy Spirit has permanently entrusted Himself to us, as shown in Ephesians 4.

> Now all of you stop putting the Holy Spirit of God in deep pain. In Him you were sealed until the day of full redemption. Every variety of bitterness, and outburst of anger, and slow burn, shouting and stupid talking, let it be taken from you with all evil (verses 30-31).

Since the Spirit of God has entrusted Himself to us, we have to be considerate of Him. We should not put Him into deep pain by the terrible way we sometimes view each other, talk about each other, and talk to each other. The word for *pain* used in Ephesians 4:30 is the same word used of Christ's torment in the Garden of

Gethsemane. Therefore, we should not continually put the Spirit of God through what Christ went through once.

℟ ℟ ℟

When our two children were young, my wife and I never left them at home alone. We did not trust them to be alone together. One time my sweet little daughter flipped my athletic son around and broke his collarbone—and that was while we were present! But God does not view us as kids. He has turned the family business over to us, and that business is to bring people into the Trinity's enjoyable circle of love. (We'll talk more about this in chapter 11.)

God is treating us as adults. He has joined Himself to us. Because we all suffer from varieties of spiritual insanity, we do not quickly see the implication: He is modeling trust so that we trust back.

God the Father does not manipulate us the way a dysfunctional person would. He doesn't say, "Produce and I'll be nice to you. Do what I want, and I'll do unto you." That is unhealthy. God, being a good Father, has really said, "I will trust you. I will ennoble you. I will treat you in a principled way, and I will be faithful to you forever because you have trusted Me a little bit. As you understand My kind of love, I will mold you into a healthy human being. I won't hurry the process, because My children are raised in a healthy way to be healthy. I do not beat them into health." God is willing to take the time to win our hearts by treating us nobly. He really trusts us.

9

God's Love—It's Not What You Think It Is

W E'VE COME A LONG WAY IN understanding how our emotions and imagination relate to each other, and how we're to manage our emotions by filling our imagination with biblical pictures of how God views us. If you've been thinking, *This all sounds too good to be true*, your thought could easily be coming from lingering suspicions about God's love. At this point in the book (as I promised in chapter 3), we need to tackle this issue. Otherwise we may experience a short-circuiting of God's plan for our emotional and relational health.

Let's lay the problem out squarely. If we ask the average Christian, "Does God love you?" the answer may well be, "Yes, He has to—that's His job." If we ask them if God likes them, the answer might well be, at best, "I hope so." They know that Jesus died for them, but they are not sure at all if He likes them or even can stand them.

False Images of God's Love

Outside of Boise, Idaho, I was with a group of 40 university students involved with Campus Crusade. We had divided them up by family backgrounds using the questionnaire I've mentioned previously. I was speaking with a dozen of them who came out of stress-filled and hurtful family backgrounds. (As usual, the leaders and the most dedicated students came out of the dysfunctional background.)

I was telling them that, although when they were growing up their parents did not comfort them or express affection for them, God the Father certainly liked them and would comfort them. All they would have to do would be to start sharing the stress and pain in their lives with Him and then ask for His comfort. Then He would comfort them some time during the same day they had asked for comfort.

Much to my surprise, they did not want to do this. They really hesitated about putting God's love and affection to the test by asking for daily comfort for the pain in their lives. When I asked why, every one of them said it would be devastating to them if they asked for comfort and He did not grant it. It would be proof that God did not deeply love them. They did not want to take the risk of asking for comfort, for God might not act. Yet the irony was that these were the most fanatical Christians in that group of 40. They would die for Jesus. They just were not sure if Jesus liked them or intensely loved them. ("Yes, God loves all people; it's just me He can't stand." That seems to be the motto of many Christians.)

The picture this very zealous group of young Christians had was that God was intermittently affectionate, and every once in a while He would bless them "somewhat." But their role was to fanatically do everything right so as to make up for the fact that God was involved only some of the time. If they more than held up their end of the bargain, every once in a while they might get a heavenly pat on the head. Therefore, when I asked them to trust God for daily comfort, it forced them to face the fact that their instinctive picture of God was not the biblical picture.

That group had a picture of an intermittently interested God. Most Christians have a slightly different picture, one like this: Hundreds and hundreds of people live in a rundown tenement in the inner city. And God is a rich philanthropist who loves to do good things. He buys the dump of a building and the block the building is on. He has the building beautifully redone and new furnishings placed in the apartments. Trees and flowers are planted all around the block. He even gives the building a new name—He calls it the "Love Building" because His love is expressed for the people through the refurbished place.

The people in the building want to know why is He doing all of this. The answer the engineers give who are redoing everything is that the rich philanthropist loves to do good things, loves people, and is buying buildings all over town to redo them to benefit the people who live in them. But, the engineers say, He does have one odd characteristic—He has no friends, He just has dependents. And He never goes fishing with the men in the buildings, nor does He chat with the women in the laundry room. In fact, He has never visited or spent any time in any of the buildings that have been redone. But the engineers keep assuring the people whose lives have been improved that the philanthropist really loves them.

God's Love in the Church at Large

In reality, God wants us to soar on an emotional life based upon a deep sense of being loved and a growing joy, with a real affection for Him and the people around us. Yet for the great majority of believers that is not the case.

As a Bible teacher working with present and future leaders, I ask the groups I have worked with, "What percentage of people in your church have a deep sense of being loved by God?" Also as part of that question I ask, "What percentage of adults in your church have an emotionally vibrant relationship with God the Father based upon what Jesus means to them?" Typical of the answers I get are "about 5 percent"; "7 percent"; "3 percent."

As I press them as to what is going on in their churches, they will describe the church members as anxious, guilty, worried, and troubled—as much that way as is the general population. In fact, I think they describe the church people as having *more* guilt and shame than the typical person outside the church.

Not one of these present and future leaders doubt their church members are receiving the right biblical truth. But something is happening between the proclamation of the truth and the integration of the truth.

I have been asking that question of leadership groups for years. The men and women who respond are from a wide range of evangelical churches and several cultural heritages: Caucasian, Asian, and black. And their answers average to 5 percent. Only 5 percent of church people appear to have any sense of being loved by God, and appear to have truth emotionally integrated into their lives!

This figure actually corresponds with the results of a 1997 study by evangelical researcher George Barna, whose organization interviews thousands of churchgoers a year:

> ❧ 67 percent of regular church attenders say they have never experienced God's presence at a church service.

❧ 48 percent of regular church attenders have not experienced God's presence in the past year anywhere.

❧ 50 percent of those who call themselves Christian rate themselves as being "absolutely committed" to the Christian faith.

Even though 50 percent of Christians are absolutely committed to the faith, a majority of them have not experienced God's presence! But this can be changed.

Part of the reason so many Christians feel unloved by God is because several definitions of love exist among Christians. One definition has love as an act of the will solely, so that God chooses to love us but basically holds His nose as He does so. Another definition is that love is a rampant romance wherein God actually really likes people and has a passionate delight in them. Let's see in the Bible what love is!

Romantic Love in the Old Testament

Come with me to a wedding feast in Israel a long time ago. We are going to a small village in Judea. It is young Miriam's village. Her fiancé, Mordecai, came with a party of friends and relatives to the village for their wedding. Feasting and dancing and romance filled the air. Nothing is so much fun as a wedding, especially an Israelite one many years ago.

Miriam and Mordecai knew each other as kids because their parents were friends and distant cousins. When the parents started to negotiate the marriage, the young couple could not have been more delighted. They really liked each other so they were excited about a future marriage. As soon as the agreement was made by the families, the couple was smothered with chaperones, and every move was watched. Nevertheless, their love grew. Just the thought of marriage turned their love into a forest fire.

The wedding party lasted a week. Food was plentiful, and every day dancing took place. It ended with a torchlight and lamplight parade to the home of the newly married couple. The real excitement, though, was the blossoming and the flourishing of love between the future husband and wife. The women thought how the couple were fixated on each other was delightful, and the men thought it was entertaining and silly. To the children who were watching and the adults who were dancing, it was obvious that Miriam and Mordecai had the real "illness." They were intensely and personally in love.

Real depths of love were present in that Israelite wedding. In their culture, a wedding and marriage had a deeply emotional and romantic side to it. This is reflected in their greatest of love songs, the Song of Songs in the Old Testament, the love poem that showed how the Israelite people looked at romance and love.

> *The essence of love is the fixated fascination that comes from the person who has had their heart captured by another.*

Such romantic love was personal, incredibly intense, and even sacrificial. The young woman who was the beloved in the poem said, "Many waters cannot quench love; neither can rivers drown it. If a man tried to buy love with everything he had, his offer would be utterly despised" (8:7).

Love is like a flame of unquenchable strength. It is so valuable that it cannot be bought. When people are in love, they can't be bribed (no matter what the amount) so as to fall in love with someone else. Their enchantment with the beloved is so intense that money and things do not matter. All things will be sacrificed for the sake of the relationship.

Among the Israelites, when someone was in love, it was more than just a romantic fling. Depth was there. In the Song of Solomon, as the lovers spoke to each other, they used various forms of endearment. The man would call his beloved his sister (5:1). He would also call her his friend (1:15) and his bride (5:1). He would even speak of her as his business partner! Further, he would speak of her as his darling (2:8 and many other times). Finally, he would call her his beloved. All of these words show how deeply love had permeated the soul. The feelings were so intense that the woman said she was sick from her love. "Strengthen me with raisin cakes. Refresh me with apples, because I am lovesick" (2:5).

The man's love was deep and complete; he was intensely focused on the person of his beloved. The essence of love is the fixated fascination of the person who has had his or her heart captured by another. Such love is intensely personal, and it easily sacrifices for another. (The experience of such love is delightful, and so is the Hebrew word for romantic love: *ahavah*. Pronounce it quickly like you are panting with love and you will land firmly on the last syllable—*aha-VAH*.)

Love Stories

In the love stories of the Old Testament we find *ahavah* expressed. The great love of the book of Genesis was the story of Jacob and Rachel. As you may remember, Jacob had to flee from his brother, Esau. He went to live with his uncle Laban. There he met and fell in love with his cousin Rachel. He asked Laban if he could marry her. And Laban said certainly, except that Jacob would have to work seven years for her! This did not discourage Jacob at all. "So Jacob served seven years for Rachel and they seemed to him but a few days because of his love *[ahavah]* for her" (Genesis 29:20 NASB). Jacob's love was intense, and it was certainly sacrificial.

After those seven years the wedding finally came, and Laban, the crafty uncle, substituted Rachel's sister Leah for Rachel. Jacob was enraged over this, for one was not the other and never could substitute for the other. He was madly in love with Rachel, and it was Rachel that he wanted.

The text tells us, "he loved Rachel more than Leah. And he served his uncle another seven years" (verse 30 NASB). *Ahavah* is the word that was used for Jacob's love, and *ahavah* is always personal. With biblical love, people are not interchangeable parts. People do not fall in love with humanity in general; they fall in love with individual persons. Jacob did not find Leah, who had the same genetic makeup as Rachel, a fit substitute. Only Rachel would do. For it was Rachel that drew the *ahavah*-love out of his heart.

Having *ahavah*-love does not make a person virtuous. A person must be virtuous first to use such a powerful passion rightly. *Ahavah* is something that comes into the life of the good and the evil. It comes with force. It comes connected to special persons in an individual's life. The good person will sacrifice nobly for the person they love, and the evil person will indeed also sacrifice. The evil person's sacrifice, however, will be tainted with wrong and folly. And it will truly cost them.

If you were able to go back in time and ask an ancient Hebrew about *ahavah*-love, these three qualities—intense, personal and passionate, and sacrificial—would certainly surface. If you asked him if you could have romantic love for just about anybody, he would think that was a strange question. In his culture *ahavah* was only for the person who had gripped the heart. If you asked him if *ahavah* was a mild emotion, he would think the question was just dumb. Romance was always intense! If you asked him if *ahavah*-love was indifferent to the needs of the beloved, he would reply that the lover might even sacrifice his life for the beloved.

God's Romance with Israel

Such intense, delighted, and sacrificial love is not just something for humans. *Ahavah* enters into the lives of not only the bad and the good, it is also part of the life of God. The God of the Old Testament experiences such love with all of its characteristics.

All of us really like to watch romantic love because it makes people beautiful. They are freed up; they are spontaneously happy. Liking and being liked romantically is one of the supreme human experiences. Yet oddly, many Christians do not connect that with God. Some churches are interested in making sure they do the right things so that God can like them and bless them. Some churches are riveted on having the right information so God can like them and bless them. But there is a third possibility. That is the dynamite possibility that Christianity is a divine romance that starts with God. The end of it is a divine romance when we respond to His passion.

In the Old Testament, people were not the only ones who experienced *ahavah*-love. *Ahavah* is also used for God's love for Israel and His own in the Old Testament. In the Bible, an Israelite could move easily from describing the romance existing between a man and a woman to describing the romance that existed between God and His people. The same elements of passion that were at our Israelite wedding showed up in God's expressed love for His own.

God's love was personal. He attached Himself to someone not because He was impressed with them, but because His love found something in them that stirred His heart! Notice what He said about Israel:

> Yahweh did not choose you and lavish His love on you because you were larger or greater than the other nations, for you were the smallest of all nations! It was simply because Yahweh loved you (Deuteronomy 7:7-8).

If Israel asked God, "Why do you love me?" the answer was simply that He did.

This love that God had for Israel was intense and enduring. God spoke through the prophet Jeremiah and said,

> Long ago Yahweh said to Israel, "Yes, I have loved you, my people, with an everlasting love. With unfailing love I have drawn you to myself" (Jeremiah 31:3).

Probably no picture of affection can surpass the affection and love that a nursing mother displays for the child at her breast. It is the universal picture of affection. God used that picture to express His own intense love for Israel, stating that His own love surpassed that of nursing mothers.

> Can a woman forget her nursing child and have no compassion on the son of her womb? Even these women may forget, but I will never begin to forget you (Isaiah 49:15).

In the real world some mothers can forget the baby at their breast (as impossible as that sounds), but God will never forget His own. It would seem foolish to ask if the newlyweds Mordecai and Miriam liked each other, or if the couple in the Song of Solomon liked each other. It would be just as foolish to ask if the nursing mother had any affection and liking for the child she was nursing. Clearly, if we say we love a particular person, it follows that we like that person.

The use of the word *ahavah* meant that God not only loved the people of Israel but intensely liked them. The great image of the nursing mother underscored that. God liked His Old Testament people. The great word for romantic love in the Old Testament was the word that God used for His love for His people. The people of the Old Testament were in a divine romance with God.

God Loves Individuals

So God's love was intense, but was it personal? Was it a love for specific individuals, or was it generic? Was it like a large, well-shaken bottle of soda—when opened, it just sprayed everyone in sight?

The book of Psalms answers that powerfully. It not only says that God knows people personally, but it rhapsodizes over how *well* He knows them.

> O Yahweh, you have searched me and know me personally. You know when I sit and when I rise; you perceive my thoughts from afar. You discern my going out and my lying down; you are familiar with all my ways. Before a word is on my tongue, you know it completely, O Yahweh (Psalm 139:1-4).

The very first verse has the Hebrew word for personal and intimate relationship. That is why I translate it "you know me personally." This personal knowledge also extended to our very existence in the womb.

You formed my inward parts; you covered me in my mother's womb. I will praise you for I am awesomely and miraculously made (Psalm 139:14-15).

Did the Israelite believe that God's love was personal and intimate? Yes, of course. But it was not love based upon one moment in time in our lives, but it was a love extended toward us through the span of our existence!

Are *We* Worth Knowing?

Is it important for us to understand that God's love is personal and not generic? Let me tell you a story. Our daughter, Adrianne, when she was 12, was going to her first school dance. This was a great event in her life, and she was preoccupied with it for weeks. The great question in her mind was, *Would any boy choose her to dance?* She desperately wanted to be chosen.

Carol, my wife, and I talked about it for weeks too. We were afraid that Adrianne might be setting herself up for deep disappointment. She got so intense about it that both of us started to pray that she would be chosen.

The evening of the dance came, and I drove her over to it. I left with my stomach probably in as many knots as Adrianne's was. I desperately wanted her to be chosen. On my way home I prayed it would happen. If I could have arranged it, I would have bribed one of those silly boys to ask her for a dance.

> *Does God like us, does He have intense feelings about us, does He find joy in us? Are we worth knowing by Him?*

Two hours later, I went back to pick her up. I did not have to ask the question. Obviously she had not been chosen.

At that point in her life, *who* chose her wasn't that important. But it was desperately important *that she be chosen.* Why? Was she concerned about who would do the choosing? Maybe a little, but her real concern was about herself. She wanted to discover if any boy her age thought she was worth knowing, if she was worth choosing, if she was worth dancing with. The issue was not the young man: The issue was herself.

My little girl was struggling with one of the most significant realities in anyone's life. Adults are far better at hiding this significant need than children, but that does not make it any less important. All of us want to know if anyone considers us worth knowing or choosing or inviting into a joy-filled relationship.

To be told that human beings are in general worth knowing, and that generically we qualify as human beings, does not help. The issue is, Is the person we are inside attractive, delightful, and loveable to somebody significant out there?

It is certainly exciting that God loved His Old Testament people so intensely and so personally. But there's a more pertinent question: Does God like *us,* does He have intense feelings about *us,* does He find joy in *us?* Are *we* worth knowing by Him? Can someone we respect and admire like us and feel passion about us? For many Christians who read their New Testament, that is a question deep in their hearts.

*Ahavah-*Love and *Agape*

I think we can answer this key question about whether God likes us individually. Let me share some information about the Bible you might not have known. The Old Testament was written between 1500 BC and 500 BC, mostly in Hebrew. But around 300 BC it was completely translated into Greek. This was the first time in the history of the world that a set of books had been translated from one language to another. A historical first! The translated set was called the Septuagint, which means *seventy* in Greek, because it was believed that 70 rabbis did the translating. (This Greek Old Testament contained a whole host of vocabulary that also showed up in the New Testament, which was also written in Greek some 300 years after the Old Testament was translated.)

These rabbis who did the translating were looking for a word in Greek for the Hebrew word *ahavah*, a word that would reflect the personal, intense liking and the willingness to sacrifice that was part of *ahavah*. They ended up doing this: Every time they came to the Hebrew verb or noun that contained *ahavah*, they translated it with the Greek word *agape*.

Whoever the rabbi was who translated the steamiest book of the Old Testament, the Song of Songs, when he came to the word *ahavah*, he used the word *agape*. When he translated the part where the man said he could not love any other woman than the one who had captured his heart, the rabbi chose *agape*. When another rabbi translated the story of Jacob and Rachel, he used *agape* because that was the only Greek word that could reflect the intense affection that was in Jacob's heart. (And whoever the rabbi was who translated the sordid story of Amnon and Tamar—2 Samuel 13:1-15—when he wanted to find a word that reflected the intense infatuation and obsession that Amnon had, he also chose *agape*.)

When other rabbis were translating the Psalms that spoke of God's love for Israel and the individual Israelite, and the love of the people for God, they chose *agape* for *ahavah* over and over again. Based on how many times *ahavah* appears in the Old Testament and how many times these rabbis translated it with *agape*, it seems obvious that for them no other word would do. *Ahavah* is always intense; it is greatly personal; and often as not, it is sacrificial. Only *agape* seemed to say the same thing as far as they were concerned. *Ahavah* means "to have a passionate delight in someone," and the rabbis believed that is what *agape* meant too. This should turn our understanding of *agape* love in the New Testament upside down!

Does God Like People?

If God does not like people but just generically loves them, then all we can feel like is an investment property. If He likes us and is passionate about us as individuals, then everything is changed. We are now in a passionate romance, a dance!

With our new understanding of God's *agape* in hand, we'll now see how one of the great sections of the New Testament answers the key question, *Does God find delight and joy in individual people?*

God's liking of people became a question and issue in the ministry of Christ. The Pharisees, the religious teachers of the Jews, were critical of Jesus because He would go to banquets where there were tax gatherers (Jewish agents of the Romans who would collect oppressive taxes) and sinners (nonpracticing Jews). They noticed that Jesus enjoyed those people. Christ spoke critically of their attitude and said,

> The Son of Man came eating and drinking, and they are saying, "Look, a glutton and a drunkard, a man who likes tax-gatherers and sinners!" Yet wisdom is justified by her results (Matthew 11:19).

What the Pharisees noticed was that Jesus acted like a friend; He acted as though He liked the people who did not conform to religious rules. The religious types were scandalized because good people shouldn't like nonreligious people—but Jesus did. The term that was used for "likes" was used in reference to either close friends or relatives. So the Pharisees were accusing Jesus of acting as though these people were likable relatives.

Jesus Answers the Question with Stories

In the Gospel of Luke, Jesus responded to this criticism with a series of three stories that are among the most famous ones in the Bible. These stories are going to answer two questions: Does God like individual persons, and when they repent, is heaven happy about it?

In Luke 15:1-2 the Pharisees were complaining about Jesus' habit of being at parties with the tax collectors and sinners. So to illustrate how heaven worked and why He was doing what He was doing, He told the stories of the lost sheep, the lost coin, and the lost son.

Most of us are familiar with the stories, but sometimes the emotional currents that are present are overlooked. The shepherd in the story left the 99 behind and went after the lost sheep. Finding it, he placed it on his shoulders while continuously rejoicing (verse 5). In the next verse he threw a party for his friends and relatives and told them to rejoice because he had found his sheep. Then Jesus said that there was more joy in heaven over one sinner who repented than the 99 who did not need to.

For three verses in a row, Jesus described how the shepherd was happy, how the friends and relatives were told to be happy, and how heaven itself was happy. Quite a contrast to the Pharisees, who were unhappy with Jesus and with the people who appeared to be His friends. The mood of the Pharisees was completely out of step with the joy in the story. Was it unrealistic for the shepherd to be so happy? No, because sheep were valuable. Also, sheep often were given names like family pets; they were liked.

What does this story tell us? First, individuals matter to Jesus and God. It was the one out of the hundred who was noticed and was sought after. Also when that one was found, it was the cause of joy all the way to heaven itself. God notices individuals, and they can make heaven happy.

In the next story, a woman lost one silver coin out of ten. It actually may have been dowry money that women sometimes sewed into their garments as decoration and a reminder of their marriage. The money was valuable and probably had sentimental value. She swept the dirt floor of her house and lit a lamp to find it. The coin mattered to her. When she found it, it caused her such joy that she threw a "mini-party" to celebrate its discovery.

Jesus made the comment that there was joy in the presence of the angels of God when one sinner repented. The phrase "joy in the presence of the angels of God" was an indirect rabbinic way of saying God was happy. (The rabbis often would use what is called circumlocution to talk about God; they would beat around the bush. They felt it was inappropriate to say God was happy, so they would say there was joy in the presence of the angels. Well, who was joyful in the presence of the angels? It was obviously God!)

Jesus accommodated Himself to their way of saying things because He wanted them to listen and did not want to needlessly offend. Again the story underscored the fact that people are valuable to God, and when they open themselves to a relationship with Him through changing their minds deeply (repentance) that makes Him happy. People can make God happy! Notice again how emotional the stories are; they have an intensity about them.

The Issue Is a Person

Next comes the most famous story of all, the story of the wasteful son, or the prodigal son. Here the numbers have come down again, from one hundred in the first story, to ten in the second, down to two. That is a nice way of saying again that the individual matters.

Of the two sons, the younger son took his inheritance and squandered it. He went off to a far country and ended up a starving pig herder. Then he repented and decided that he would return home. As he neared home his father saw him from a great distance. The dad felt deep compassion for his son and ran to him, threw his arms around him, and repeatedly kissed him.

Notice that the father's heart was attached to his son while the son was far away. While that son had made himself "relationally dead," the son was in his father's thoughts and deeply mattered to him. The father's eyes were glued to the distance longing for his son's return. Did the father stop feeling for his son while the son was away? Did the father stop passionately loving his son?

The obvious answers are, he did not. Driven by compassion and affection, he ran. His feet expressed his yearning, and his kisses expressed his longing. Then he also threw a party to express his love!

What if, as the father was running towards his son, we stopped him to ask some questions:

"Are you running so fast because your son is repenting and you want to make sure he doesn't change his mind?"

"No!" he answers.

"Are you running fast so you can start instructing him on how to live a godly life?"

Again he answers, "No!"

So we ask again why he is running so fast and why tears are streaming down his face.

He shouts at us as he starts running again, "Because it is my son and I love him!"

We shout after him, "But you have two sons, so why are you running?"

From a ways off we hear, "Because I love him."

The next sound we hear is sobbing in the distance.

The older, religious brother, who was like the Pharisees, was upset. In effect he said, "What does liking have to do with it?" When the father threw a big party, slaughtered the fattened calf, gave the younger son a robe, put a ring on his finger, and sandals on his feet, the older brother did not like it. Refusing to go to the party, he stewed at a distance. The dad, who would not chase his younger son into the far country, chased after this older son. For the older brother was in greater spiritual danger than the younger son ever was. The older brother's attitude was, "I've kept the rules and he hasn't—and that is all there is to it." The older brother thought life revolved around keeping rules and not around love and relationships.

He complained to his father and said, "I have never broken one of your rules, but as soon as this son of yours who wasted his money on prostitutes comes back, you throw a party for him!" The father said, "It's a necessity to rejoice and be glad, because your brother was dead and now is alive. He was completely lost and he is found!"

What is behind the father's emotional reactions through this story? Obviously he passionately loved his younger son (as well as the older one). The issue for the father was not what the son had done wrong—the issue was the son! The father's great affection for his son made the party necessary.

This story was designed to explain to the Pharisees how heaven operates and how Jesus acts. It and the stories of the shepherd and the woman were told so as to open the door of heaven, so that we and the Pharisees could peek in. What we see is that heaven's God values people and becomes emotional when they go from relational death to life. God is happy because He and they can have a relationship.

Jesus was saying through the story that going to these banquets (parties) was necessary because He loved and liked and was passionate about these individual tax collectors and sinners. He thought He should go to those parties to celebrate the new relationship between His Father and that tax collector or that sinner. He went because He liked them! Does God the Father feel the same way? Obviously heaven's God does, because Jesus used the joy in heaven to justify His own behavior.

Talking Themselves out of Being Loved

Many Christians have the attitude that God *has* to do this salvation thing; it is His job description. They do not seem convinced that God loves them passionately. This attitude about God's *agape* love, that God is obligated to love—almost like there are rules that force him to do so—is common among the children of God.

As a Bible teacher, I have seen this refusal to be loved crop up in many different ways. Let me give you some illustrations. If I am teaching a small group Bible study about Christ dying for our sins, the listeners more often than not interpret that to mean that He despises our sins more than He loves us. They seem to feel that the reason Christ died for sins was not to rescue those He loves but to deal with an accounting mess in the universe. The books of the universe desperately needed balancing, so the Son of God died to deal with the crisis.

People seem to shy away from the question of God liking and delighting in them because of the same fear my daughter had at the sixth-grade dance—maybe no one can find anything in us worth liking. That is a dreadful fear, and a common one.

So when Christians hear about Christ dying for them they confuse the means with the end. The *means* are the suffering of Christ, but the *goal* is to establish a relationship with us. All too often, they make the means everything. God had necessarily to deal with sin, but they forget that His real goal was to establish a friendship with us.

It is almost like Christians have an "anti-liking gun" in their heads, and when a thought that God might possibly like them wings its way toward their heart, they blow it out of the air!

As another example, I am always teaching about our identity in Christ because I think it is one of the most freeing teachings in the Bible. When the heart gets hold of that truth, the human soul takes flight! But more often than not, the "anti-liking gun" starts shooting. People will ask questions like this:

> ❦ "Doesn't God put us in Christ so that we and our sin can be covered up?"
>
> ❦ "Doesn't God put us in Christ so that He can love Christ in us?"
>
> ❦ "Isn't being put in Christ something like being painted with whitewash so that God doesn't have to see us?"

I always ask them to turn to Ephesians 2:4-6. Then, I ask them some questions after I read this to them:

> God, being rich in mercy, because of His great passionate love with which He passionately loved us, even when we were corpses in our trespasses, made us alive together with Christ (by grace you are being permanently saved), and raised us up with Him, and seated us with Him in the upper heavens.

The first question I ask them: "What came first, His mercy or His love?" They usually answer, "Well since His mercy was on account of His great *agape* love, His love must have come first."

Second question: "Was His *agape* love great or just average?" They usually answer, "It was great."

Third question: "Did our being joined with Christ make us loved, or were we placed into Christ because He first loved us?" They usually answer, almost with a look of surprise on their faces, "His love for us placed us in Christ."

> *God's desire was not to hide us away but to join us to the Son of His love.*

It is God's *agape* love that is driving His mercy, that led to the cross, and that has placed us in His Son. Our identity in Christ and His mercy did not twist God's heavenly arm to love us. His passionate delight in us—His *ahavah*-love, His *agape* for you and me—led to our being joined to Christ!

What drives the work of salvation? It is God's passionate delight for us. Out of His great love for us, He is rich in mercy. Out of His great love for us, He has joined us to His Son. Because He loves us, He has joined us to the Son He infinitely loves. That gives us a new family identity instead of our checkered history of shame and guilt. So the result is that when He looks at His Son in heaven, He sees us. When He looks at us on earth, He sees the Son. God's desire was not to hide us away but to join us to the Son of His love. That way His love for us is expressed by an incredible gift, the gift of being joined to the Son.

❧ ❧ ❧

The Picture of a Dad

When Jesus' heart was in turmoil while He was in the Garden of Gethsemane, He turned to heaven and said, *"Abba...*Dad...*"* Experiencing God's *agape* love starts with understanding God as a "Dad." That has to become a rich source of emotional strength within. A most effective way to work with our own emotions is, first understand the doctrine biblically, from the text; then take emotionally significant images and play those images through our mind, using our imagination, to view God as an affectionate Father.

So in my own mind, I view God the Father as a Dad who is running to meet His children. He's smiling, He's grabbing them up into His arms, and He's dancing with them—He's enjoying them. When I see a healthy father responding in a gracious and kind way to his children, I take that image, play around with it, and say, "That's what God is like." We need to *feel* these emotionally rich truths.

That's what language is supposed to do—feed the imagination. We need to function like poets, using the imagination to grapple with the truth of God's passionate delight for us. When we're delighted with the picture of His love in our imagination, we should turn to Him and say, "I'm grateful You're like that."

10

The Model for Life

WHEN I DO SEMINARS, every so often I will invite people to give me a call if they want to talk about what they have learned or if they want to be coached. One attendee did that, and we sat down for a conversation at my office.

Without hesitating he launched into his story. "When I was young my parents traveled all over the world. They were very serious Christians, and I became a Christian young. For me their traveling was a lonely experience, and I filled in the time with pornography, masturbation, and all-around sex."

This appeared to be a well-rehearsed story for him so I figured he must have previously been in counseling or pastoral care. (A person who has not been in counseling tells their story in an entirely different way; it's more like a messy travelogue.) Over the next 20 minutes, he unblushingly described his sexually addictive lifestyle. Then, poking at the air to make his points, he said that when his family returned to the United States, he thought he should get married. "I felt that would cure me of this addiction," he commented, "but it did not work. I was as addicted as ever. I was getting involved with prostitutes, and now I have gotten involved with another woman."

His wife got outraged with him and threw him out of the home, and now she was in a relationship with another man. As he finished his story, he looked at me with a glance that said, *It's your turn and this better be good.*

Over the years I have taken a few pages out of Jesus' approach and practiced His "rhetoric of crisis," which He uses so effectively in the Sermon on the Mount. Part of that rhetoric is to say the unexpected and to ask the person to do the unexpected. So I said, "I have only one thing to say and ask: Have you shown the centerfolds to God?"

He froze in place. His eyes fixed themselves on me.

"I am very serious," I said, and I repeated the question: "Have you shown the centerfolds to God the Father?"

He blushed. He did not blush when he described pornography, fornication, and adultery, but with that question he blushed! I started laughing and said, "You're blushing!" He blushed even more.

"That's the whole problem," I went on. "You don't believe you can show the centerfold to God. He's about the only one you can and should. Whether it is the centerfold in the magazine or the centerfold in your imagination, God the Father is the one you should show it to."

Sorting Things Out

I went on to tell him that the greatest compliment a son could give a father is to go to his dad with the pictures and struggles in his heart and mind. I told him he should take those pictures into the Father's presence and sort out his moods and desires there. I also told him he could and should do that because of the blood of Christ:

> Having then, brethren, free and friendly access to enter the
> holy place by the blood of Jesus, by a new and living way
> that He opened for us through the veil, that is, His flesh, and
> since a great priest is over the house of God, let us draw near
> with a truth-filled heart with the deep confidence of faith,
> having our hearts sprinkled from an evil conscience and our
> bodies washed with pure water (Hebrews 10:20-22).

Through the blood of Christ, the addicted man could take what troubled him into God's holy presence and sort it out. We then talked some more, and he thanked me and went on his way.

But that is not the end of the story. Several months later, I was visiting a church to speak with a pastor right after the Sunday morning church service. As I was waiting in the foyer, a man with a beard, holding a woman's hand, walked up to me with a big grin on his face. I did not recognize him at all. He kept smiling at me, and I thought, *That's the problem with giving seminars—too many people recognize my face and I don't recognize theirs.* With an even bigger grin, he said, "Since I last saw you I grew a beard. I'm the guy you told to show the centerfold to God." Last time I had seen him he had blushed; this time I blushed. You don't say that kind of thing in a church foyer! I looked around nervously and hoped he wouldn't speak so loudly.

He then went on to say he'd started practicing exactly what I'd told him, and it had made a massive difference. He was now managing his sexuality, and his sex drives were not dominating him. Then I wondered, *Who is this woman whose hand he is holding?* I pastored for 16 years before going into seminary and seminar work. Because of that experience, I thought he was going to tell me next that God had led him to dump his wife, who was angry with him, and that this was his new girlfriend. Instead he told me that this was his wife. She was smiling broadly. He had told her what I had told him. She had agreed to give him another chance, and things were working out beautifully.

After meeting them at the church, I would usually run into them once a year over the next five years or so. Each time they would tell how they were growing together in the Lord, and how much they appreciated the truth I had told the husband.

Recapturing the Imagination

This man was practicing was what we have learned so far. He had applied what we have been learning to the mood and sin cycle. He had found that God the Father would tremendously help a person who applied the truth of our identity with Christ and the access that provides. That is what all of us need to learn and apply. That is what we will see how to do in this chapter.

The addicted man had been defining himself by his failure— and not by what Christ had done for him. As he suffered more and more defeat in dealing with his sexuality, the more he defined himself as a hopeless sex addict. This prevented him from going to God the Father with the detailed pictures in his mind and in the midst of his sexually immoral acts, and this prevented him from getting the help he needed.

He needed to define himself the way God the Father sees him. The Father sees him suffering with Christ for his sexual sin; the Father sees him dying with Christ to his past; the Father sees him being raised with Christ to a new kind of life. The Father is granting to him through the blood of Christ the same quality of access that Jesus the Son has.

Further, the man was living off a massive warehouse of X-rated videotapes that were stored in his imagination and heart.

When he tried to avoid one picture, another would just pop into his mind. Instead of trying to practice avoidance, he should have been taking them into the Father's presence so he could learn how to view and handle them in a mature way. Avoidance does not build character, but sorting these things out with God the Father does. As we share enticing pictures with the Father, in a wonderful and powerful way the Holy Spirit blunts the power of the picture, gives us peace, and gives us a new perspective. (That perspective is much different than that of a teenage boy hiding in his bedroom, preoccupied with sex.)

The Area of Sexuality

Is dealing with sexually-explicit material a problem just for males? Not at all! We were doing an "Addiction Proofing Your Life and Family" seminar in the California Bay Area. We spoke about how Satan attacks men through the sexual appetite to defeat them in the spiritual life, and how he attacks women through the appetite for food and their concern about body image and appearance. We started getting notes from a small group of women who were irritated with us because we seemed to be saying that sexual addiction and fantasy were only problems for men. (Really we don't say that. Instead we say that both men and women struggle with food and sexual issues alike, but in general men struggle with sexuality and women with the appetite for food.)

I decided to address the issue in the part of the seminar where one of our women lecturers would talk about her struggle with anorexia and how the principles we've talked about changed her life. I started the lecture by holding up a brown-paper bag. I told the audience that on my way there I had stopped off at a major supermarket and looked for a pornographic men's magazine. As

I'd expected, there was not one in the store. Then I went looking for the women's romance paperbacks. I found a wall stretching 30 feet filled with them. Twenty years ago the pictures on the covers would have been considered "light porn." I bought one and took it to the seminar in the brown-paper bag. As I took the book out, I said that the text in the novels was designed to inflame the imagination, the same way the pictures in the men's magazine were.

In either case, as I shared with the women and men at the seminar, we have to take the plots of the books and the pictures in our imaginations to God to sort out. Our imagination matters. The imagination that can be filled with the sexually explicit should be filled with how the Father sees us.

The Two Choices We Have

What we have just talked about is the heart of dealing with the mood and sin cycle. Earlier in this book we examined how temptation, compulsion, and addiction work. We saw that strong and powerful emotions, often painful ones, can be dealt with by using the desires to bring some pleasure and to kill the emotional pain. The man with the centerfold was killing the loneliness of his younger years with mismanaged sexuality. But pornography is not a healthy cure for loneliness or sadness for men. And many women kill the loneliness of their marriages with romance novels. Both sexes do not realize they may be also killing their marriages or their chances for healthy future relationships.

To review the mood cycle briefly (see chapter 2 for more detail), the painful emotions are dealt with by succumbing to some desire, and that leads to sin. After the satisfaction that comes from desire, or lust, dissipates, the painful emotion returns and the cycle starts all over.

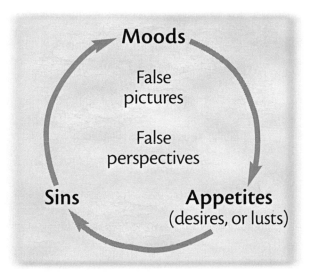

Just as we saw previously, Paul the apostle was very aware of this cycle, and he referred to the twin elements of it. For example, in Galatians 5:22 he wrote,

> Now those who belong to Christ Jesus have crucified the system of the flesh with its strong painful emotions and appetites.

Notice the two terms used: "strong painful emotions" and "appetites." The Greek word for "strong painful emotions" can be used of physical suffering (such as the suffering of Christ), or the emotional suffering that comes upon a person, as it is here. The word for "appetites" is the normal Greek word for wanting something. It is the context that tells us whether the first word is referring to physical or emotional suffering, and whether the second word is referring to a good use of appetite or a bad one. When joined to the term "system of the flesh," both words are used in a negative sense.

The system of the flesh is our identification with our old man and his appetites, and with our life outside of Christ. (We translate it as "system of the flesh" because of the fact that it is the flesh *system* that is killed with Christ—not our human body, or flesh.) All of that has been nullified in our identity with Christ and our new birth. We are free of that system, and we can walk in a new kind of life. Though that system has been destroyed, our emotions and appetites remain. We can either manage them through a living relationship with God the Father...or we can simply recycle old ways of looking at ourselves, God, and the world, and act as enslaved as we were before we trusted in Christ.

> *We can take the emotions and desires and pictures into the Father's presence and stay there until we get them sorted out.*

So let's put all of this together. When we find ourselves with a painful emotion, we have two choices:

- ❧ *We can talk it through with God and other people.* The Father sees us identified with His Son, joined to the central events of His life. With that identification, we are liberated from the past pictures and videos. We can take the emotions and desires and pictures into the Father's presence and stay there until we get them sorted out.

- ❧ *We can let the discomfort fester until we are forced to do something about it.* That "something" usually means finding an appetite to drown the painful emotion in. The emotion and the appetite will usually come with video clips— that is, with images of previous temptations and failures. We can let those clips play themselves in our imagination with their accompanying powerful emotions of worthlessness, guilt, and shame.

Starting with the Imagination

As we saw above, we can choose to focus on the video clips of past defeats, emotionally charged scenes, or anything else that distorts our vision so we do not see God, ourselves, and the world in a healthy way. For instance, it may be pictures from a childhood of verbal, physical, and sexual abuse that really define how a person sees the world. In fact, often as not an abuse victim has a frightened child's view of the world in their heart. Those pictures then create the "world" that an addiction will live in.

Those pictures in the heart also fuel the mood cycle. (Take another look at the diagram on page 205.) To effectively deal with the mood cycle we have to start at the top, and the pictures that are in our imagination will either give us permission to go to God the Father for help, or they will hinder us.

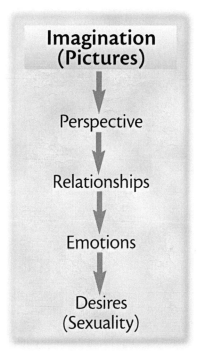

What we have seen throughout this book is that the pictures we carry around in our hearts have a profound influence on how we manage our emotions and appetite. God has created us in such a way that the pictures that we consciously or unconsciously choose will have a profound effect on our inner life. And He has created us to operate from our imagination on down.

Recapturing the Perspective for God

Beneath what is in our imagination are our *perspectives,* which can be biblical or unbiblical. When our perspectives are unhealthy, they are the self-serving excuses we give ourselves so we can continue in the mood or addiction cycle. The woman who is endlessly reading romance novels tells herself that, even if she worked at making herself more attractive for her husband, he would not care or notice. Or she has unaddressed bitterness that justifies her flight into a nonexistent world of romance. A husband who is gambling justifies it because he is doing it out of love for his family. When he makes it big, he tells himself, he will be able to take care of them. The perspective is whatever excuse allows the person to indulge the flesh.

Sometimes a married couple may have two different addictions that feed on each other. A husband might have a pornography habit, and the wife will drown her relational sorrows in food. Then the husband's excuse for continuing his habit is the wife's appearance and weight. The wife's excuse is that, due to her husband's inattention, she has every right to satisfy her appetite for food. The perspective the couple has adopted makes them very vulnerable, but at the same time it gives them the excuse they need to continue the addictive behavior.

The pictures that feed addiction need to be challenged with the new pictures that the Bible provides. The perspective that feeds addiction needs to be replaced with a biblical viewpoint. The negative pictures of the past need to be replaced with how the Father views us, and the perspective has to become healthy.

Often as not, the old perspective is there to shore up fear of change. When a person gets into the rut of the mood cycle, the heart begins to believe that is all there is in life. When a person who is living off anxiety hears about the peace God could provide, the fear of change keeps the person from trying a spiritual alternative.

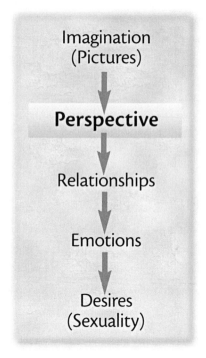

God's Ways Are Beneficial

Below the new *pictures* of our union with Christ has to be added the *perspective* that God's new ways are positively good and greatly beneficial. God's perspective benefits us. What keeps people from embracing the gospel, and what keeps Christians from embracing a life of godliness, is the fear they will lose whatever pleasure they have for some undefined good that God promises. So the perspective the Christian needs to switch to is that to embrace God's will is to embrace that which is good.

But the good can only be experienced after the practice of faith and obedience. The New Testament builds a foundation for faith by going out of its way to encourage us that God has nothing but good intentions towards us:

> What then shall we say to these things? Since God (is) on our behalf, who (is) against us? He who did not spare His own unique Son, but handed Him over for us all, how will He not also with Him graciously grant us all things? (Romans 8:31-32).

The simple reality is, if God gave a Son for us, then everything else has to be small change. His intentions towards us are wonderfully positive, and His plan throughout eternity is to be kind to us. We have seen that our union with Christ has this goal: "in order that in the ages to come He might show the surpassing riches of His grace in kindliness toward us in Christ Jesus" (Ephesians 2:7). God's intention is to be kind to us in time and be kind to us throughout all eternity.

That is the perspective we need so that we will aggressively deal with our moods and appetites. God has something more profoundly satisfying for us than just satisfying a desire. Paul encouraged us to make life an exploration of God's goodness. The exploration will lead us to experience true benefit from the Lord's provision for our lives. Notice the three critical terms that are used to describe the Lord's will:

> I am encouraging you, brethren, by the tender mercies of God, to immediately present your bodies a living and holy sacrifice, acceptable to God, (which is) your spiritual priestly

service. And stop being conformed to this age, but be inwardly transformed by the qualitative renewal of your mind, so that you may be putting to the test what the settled desire of God is for you, that which is *beneficial* and *pleasing* and *complete* (Romans 12:1-2).

Chapters 1 through 8 of Romans describe how God sees us and how we should live based upon our union with Christ. Then Romans 12:1-2 describes the perspective a believer should have. Instead of living by what the culture tells us, we are to have our thinking qualitatively renewed.

Then we can enter the grand experiment of discovering the will of God. Paul tells us that if we submit ourselves to God, we can start putting God's settled desires to the test. It is not that God is testing us, but rather that we are to test out the suitability of God's will. As we do that, the will of God should become beneficial, pleasing, and complete in our perspective.

As we continue to obey the Lord and submit ourselves to Him, our minds will become convinced of three things:

1. *What God wants for us is beneficial to us.* God the Father wants us to experience the freedom of being able to manage our emotions and appetites. As we address emotions such as anxiety, depression, worthlessness, and shame in a living relationship with God where our feelings really are spiritual issues, we will discover that making spiritual issues out of our emotions is beneficial. We will see anxiety become peace, and guilt become a fresh feeling of innocence. As our negative emotions lose their clout, then our desires will be much easier to manage—another benefit.

2. *What God wants for us will be pleasing.* Not only will God be delighted, we too will be delighted!

3. *What God wants for us will be complete*—that is, it will fit us wonderfully well. The word *complete* implies that we will have a sense we have not missed out on life. Life with God will bring a completeness we have never experienced before.

These qualities of being beneficial, pleasing, and complete will become our opinion of the will of God. Instead of being "salesmen and saleswomen" for God, we will be delighted customers.

A Fresh Perspective on Pain

Janie is a carrier of a rare genetic disorder. As a result, over the years she lost four baby boys within a week or two of their births. The doctors felt that the disease was treatable so they kept encouraging her desire to have more children. After the fourth baby's death, she was a wreck.

Janie had become a Christian in her teenage years. She and her husband, Mike, faithfully participated in the life of the church and learned the Bible. Unfortunately, as she was going through this tragedy, she fell into thinking there must be some sin in their lives because this was happening. Her own sense of failure and guilt, combined with bad and thoughtless advice, put her into a deep depression. She started to misuse prescription drugs and alcohol.

I once was asked to visit the home Bible study she was in. She had endless questions and appeared to be deeply suspicious of the ways of God. Obviously, she had every right to be. As she spent more time in the Bible study, though, she entrusted herself more and more to God the Father. She began to believe the pictures in the Bible, and she placed herself in them. She pictured God the Father walking her to the cross after He found her guilty and ashamed over the death of the babies. In her mind she saw God the Father pointing to His dying Son on the cross as the expression of the immensity of His love for her. She viewed herself as joined to the Son and the central events of the Son's life. She started to define herself as a daughter of God, and not the product of tragedy. That had an immediate effect on her emotions.

Janie's desire for alcohol and prescription drugs started to steadily decline, and she continually had the desire to help and encourage people who had been devastated by life's tragedies. As she participated more and more in addressing the needs of those struck down by tragedy, she began to experience the sense that God's will for her was beneficial, pleasing, and complete. Out of deep heartache, a deep ministry was developing in her life.

Two Key Points About Perspective in Suffering

Janie was allowing her perspective to be formed by the Bible's unique approach to suffering. Part of the privilege of being a believer is to conform our lives to the suffering of Christ and to experience life as He did. Our perspective needs to reflect two truths about suffering. The first is that profound and positive character change occurs through it, and the second is that heavenly rewards are gained through it.

> We do not allow our hearts to enter an evil condition, but though our outer person is continually decaying, yet our inner person is being qualitatively renewed day by day. For momentary, light affliction is producing for us an eternal weight of glory far beyond all comparison, while we look not at the things that are seen, but at the things that are not seen; for the things that are seen are temporary, but the things that are not seen are eternal (2 Corinthians 4:16-18).

This is the wondrous reality. If we accept the suffering life brings us, don't succumb to burying pain with pleasure, and trust

God through them, the two great things we mentioned above will become true in our lives. But we must choose to look through our tears and beyond the tragedy in front of us to eternal realities: our relationship to God the Father, and our hope of heaven.

The first reality we will experience is, as we deal with the emotional pain and tragedy of life through faith instead of addictive behaviors sprouting up within us, *we will be deeply changed within.* The text says we will be "qualitatively renewed day by day." The word for *new* means "new in quality, or qualitatively fresher and fresher." As our bodies deteriorate and we become older, within our spirits we will become younger and younger.

The second reality is that *our present light afflictions will become the source of an eternal weight of glory.* When Paul the apostle referred to "light affliction," in the context he was referring to being stoned, being whipped, being anxious, and other sufferings (2 Corinthians 11:21-33). Obviously he was using irony. He said that such sufferings will produce—or more accurately, cultivate or grow—an eternal weight of glory that simply cannot be compared to the initial sufferings. If some of the sufferings of this life seem to be monumentally overwhelming, then how much more gargantuan must be the glorious reward.

Looking Forward to God's Glorious Transmutation

In the New Testament, Jesus Christ manifested His glory by miracles. For example, in John 2 Jesus showed His glory by changing water into wine. As the servants poured the water from the purification jars, they became wine as it flowed into the wine jugs.

> This miracle was in Cana of Galilee when He first manifested His glory, and His disciples believed on Him (verse 11).

What was glorious was how Christ took mere water and turned it into the best wine. Both the water and the wine were fluids, and the wine came from the water. A relationship existed between the two of them. The observers could not help but notice the connection. God glorifies Himself when He takes the common things or tragedies of life and turns them into magnificent eternal realities.

In John 11, Jesus healed a man born blind. The question had been asked of Him why this man had been born blind. Jesus answered that he had been born blind so as to display the glory of God. Again part of the display of glory is the fact the blindness and the ability to see were related. When God or Christ displayed their glory, they would take a common condition or catastrophe and change it into something wonderful. Yet one could perceive a direct connection between the initial challenge and the glorious result (John 11:4,40). Nonetheless, if we approached the man born blind and asked him how he would compare his blind state and his seeing state, he would probably say there was no comparison. It was beyond all comparison, even though a connection existed.

When God displays His glory, He is taking something humble and changing it into something magnificent. This we can see in the resurrection and glorification of Jesus Christ. He is the same Person before and after His resurrection and glorification. Yet His glorious reign and presence in heaven infinitely outstrip His humble ministry on earth.

What Paul was emphasizing in all this was that when we are engulfed by tragedy, we should not use our desires to kill pain and ignore the spiritual challenge. "We do not allow our hearts to enter an evil condition" (2 Corinthians 4:16). Instead, through faith we should look to eternal realities. As we do, our inner life will be changed, and we will amass a wondrous eternal reward.

Whatever is the problem that you may be struggling with now, if you look through your tears to your Father in heaven in faith, you will meet that problem again. But it will be in heaven, and the problem will be changed, glorified, and given to you as an eternal gift by God. You will see a direct relationship with the problem you struggled with on earth. Yet in heaven, you will never be tempted to make a comparison between the problem and God's display of glory. Any comparison will be ludicrous.

> As I looked...to eternal realities, I found a "Dad" in heaven, an elder brother in Jesus, and the help and encouragement of the Spirit of God.

Janie lost four baby sons. She has come to a resolution in her heart that she will trust God with that problem and use it as a way to help and encourage others who are going through tragedy. God the Holy Spirit, as a result, is renewing her heart day by day. And when she and her husband, Mike, enter heaven, the God of endless creativity and infinite power will have taken their tears and turned them into spiritual diamonds of great weight and worth, so to speak. Possibly she and Mike will have the joy and privilege of a special relationship to those four sons now glorified in heaven. However God does it, throughout eternity Janie will be able to say that God indeed has made it up to her, and how He did it was so wonderful that it cannot be compared to the original tragedy.

Several times I have mentioned my growing up in an alcoholic home. Later in adult life I would think about what a waste that was. Those who have been raised in alcoholic homes or homes of addicts often have never had a childhood. For me, life was never carefree or stress-free. But over time several wonderful things have happened. As I looked beyond the pain of those years to eternal realities, I found a "Dad" in heaven, an elder brother in Jesus, and the help and encouragement of the Spirit of God. Deep changes started happening. My heart was qualitatively renewed over and over again—so much so that as I got older, I felt younger and younger (a reverse aging process, if you will). Second, I found that those painful experiences gave me a deep insight into what people actually go through—and as the Lord helped me, I was able to help them. Lastly, I have the joy of looking forward to heaven to see what God will do with the pains of this life. It will be breathtaking to see how He takes tragedy and turns it into an eternal weight of glory. This will be the ultimate new perspective!

Recapturing Relationships

Imagination and perspective create the stage for *relationships*. We set the stage by how we picture God, the world, and ourselves. The pieces of furniture on the stage are the perspectives we have on life. Relationships are how we then respond to God and react to others on the stage.

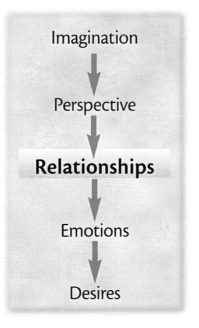

In the first ten verses of Romans 6, Paul describes how God sees us immersed into the Person of Christ and the central events of Christ's life. Then in verse 11 we are commanded to assume that we are continually alive to God in Christ Jesus. We are to assume we have ever-constant access to God the Father, by which we can come into His presence and receive the same reception He gives to Jesus.

Based upon those pictures and spiritual perspectives, we are to sort out our relationship with God the Father and sort out life. What are the kinds of things we are to address? First and foremost, the emotional issues of life.

Being Captivated by Our Relationship with God

Any good dad would want his children to come to him with their concerns and fears. Almost anything can qualify as an issue to be sorted out with our heavenly Father. As Peter wrote,

> Immediately humble yourselves therefore under the incredibly powerful hand of God, that He may exalt you at the right time; be continually throwing all your anxiety upon Him, because it is a concern to Him about you (1 Peter 5:6-7).

In other words, if it matters to you, it matters to Him.

As an example, the sorts of things we are to talk to the Father about in our new relationship to Him are contained in the Lord's Prayer in Matthew. This is an illustration of what I would call "issues-oriented prayer." Prayer, or relating to God, the Father in the Bible is not a matter of time, schedule, and technique. It is simply sorting out with a good Dad the important and unimportant concerns of life.

The Pharisees, the religious teachers of Christ's time, built their relational life with God around a rigid schedule:

> Whenever you pray, you are not to be as the hypocrites; for
> they really like to stand and pray in the synagogues and on
> the street corners, in order to be seen by men. Truly I say to
> you, they are receiving their reward in full (Matthew 6:5).

Typically they prayed three times a day, and whenever it came
time for prayer, wherever they were they stopped and prayed.
Prayer became a public performance rather than a private conversation with God. Jesus said that the performance was reward
enough for them.

Nor is a relationship with God based on a lot of words. When
Jesus was teaching about prayer in the Sermon on the Mount,
He said prayer was not an issue of quantity.

> When you are praying, do not use meaningless repetition,
> as the Gentiles do, for they suppose that they will be heard
> for their many words (Matthew 6:7).

A Place to Sort Out the Issues

So relating to God the Father is not a scheduled exercise or a
laundry-list exercise (because He knows already what we need);
nor is it a "wearing down" of God by words. Relating to God is
sorting out the issues of life with a good Father. The Lord's Prayer
gives a series of issues that really defines our relationship with
God. The prayer begins, "Our Father, the One in heaven, let your
Name be set apart." It puts words in the mouth of the person who
is praying, asking God to help the person see and understand His
Fatherhood. So the first issue in the Lord's Prayer is making sure
our understanding and perception (our pictures) are right.

Then another issue is expressed by asking God the Father that
His will would be done on earth as in heaven (Matthew 6:10).
And obviously, as we grapple with the issue of the Father's will,

we also have to grapple with our perspective as to its beneficiality for us, as we discussed earlier.

Then comes the issue of our daily needs. "Daily bread" was the most common sustenance that people needed in the ancient world. So another thing we can talk to the Father about is our own needs.

Our relationships with others are also brought to the surface by having us say to God that the way He forgives us should be based upon how we forgive others (verse 12). That makes our relationships to others and forgiving others a major priority.

The last issue in the Lord's prayer is to request deliverance from temptation and the evil one, the devil (verse 13). With that prayer we recognize the stunning reality that Satan cannot go beyond what God allows.

In summary, the issues are those of

- setting apart our Abba Father in heaven
- wanting the Father's will
- small and great provisions
- our relationships with others
- being attacked by Satan

These are the kinds of things that should be brought into our relationship with the Father. It is in prayer where the pictures in our hearts and the perspectives in our minds become hugely important.

Our Relationship with the Holy Spirit

When it comes to the life of the emotions and desires, God's ministry to us has to be apportioned among the three Persons of the Trinity. When we are struggling with painful emotions and strong, enslaving appetites, we talk them through with the Father. We bring into His presence the feelings, the desires, the pictures or negative "video clips" from our past, and our self-serving perspectives, and we sort them out with Him.

The Son is always involved in a different way. He supplies the access for the conversation. Through the identity we have with Christ and the provision of His blood, we are accepted the way the Son is accepted.

The Spirit of God's ministry to our emotions is given the name "walking by means of the Spirit." To put this in perspective, when we sketch out the work of the Father, Son, and Holy Spirit in the book of Romans, the members of the Trinity are progressively introduced in their various ministries:

- Romans 3:21-24—the Son is our payment for sins
- Romans 5:1-11—the Son is our identity
- Romans 6:11-14—the Father is the One we relate to
- Romans 8:1-14—the Spirit gives us the ability to have a spiritual walk

In other words, the Father is our "Dad" in heaven, the Son gives us an identity before the Father, and the Spirit grants us His fruit in our emotional lives and our lives in the world. The Son changed our status before the Father, and the Spirit changes our emotional life in the presence of the Father,

> so that the requirement of the Law might be fulfilled in us, who do not organize their lives (walk) according to the flesh but according to the Spirit. For those who are organizing their lives according to the flesh set their perspectives on the things of the flesh, but those who are organizing their lives according to the Spirit, the things

of the Spirit. For the perspective set on the flesh is a state of death, but the perspective set on the Spirit is *life and peace* (Romans 8:4-6).

Walking by Means of the Spirit

Walking by means of the Spirit is organizing our inner world and outer world around the emotional qualities the Spirit provides. His ministry is to transition us from the moods and desires of the flesh to the emotions and relationships of love, joy, and peace. (We talked about these foundational Christian emotions more in depth in chapter 4.) We can see the difference between the flesh and the Spirit in the emotions in Romans 8:6 above. If we build our lives around the flesh, we experience relational death with God. If we build our lives around the Spirit, we experience real life and peace.

Several years ago I was deeply disappointed by the treatment my wife and I received from some Christian friends. I had made a career choice they did not like, and so they washed us out of their lives. We apologized to them about everything we could think of, but they were not satisfied. I felt wretched and betrayed and thought bitterly to myself, *I guess we are not worth their forgiveness.* It hurt even more because I felt we had not really done anything wrong.

I was so hurt, bitter, and angry that I really did not want to pray about it. But I realized I was accepted through Christ, so I told the Father about my anger and bitter emotions. I told Him I was so angry that I really did not want to forgive the couple or talk about the whole thing. Gradually over a period of weeks, I started to discuss my feelings. Gradually the Spirit prompted me to tell more and more to the Father. Because of my acceptance in Christ, I eventually told the Father everything about it. As I did, my emotions changed until I could forgive and be at peace. I spoke to the

Father through my identity in the Son—and my inner life was helped, encouraged, and empowered by the Spirit.

Moving Us Out of the Flesh

Putting it in other terms, the Spirit of God will transition us from the works of the flesh (like my bitterness) to His fruit:

> I am continually saying, organize your life around spiritual qualities, and you will never carry out a desire of the flesh. For the flesh sets its desire against the Spirit, and the Spirit against the flesh; for these are set in opposition to one another, in order that you may not do the things that you desire (Galatians 5:16-17).

The Spirit's ministry is to negate the flesh. In our inner life, they have been set in opposition to each other. God the Father has sent a divine Person to handle our appetites and emotions. He has set the Spirit in our inner life to oppose any attack of the flesh with its moods and strong desires. At any point of temptation or overwhelming emotion, we can go to the Father.

Paul goes on to give us a lengthy list of the things the Spirit can help us with. They are all described as works of the flesh:

> …sexual immorality, dirty-mindedness, and indecency, idolatry, sorcery, hatred, strife, jealousy, outbursts of anger, disputes, dissensions, factions, envying, drunkenness, carousing, and things like these (Galatians 5:19-21).

All of these different inner conditions can be changed by the Spirit. We can transition from intense sexual pressure to do something immoral to peace, love, and self-control from the Spirit. Or if the issue is relational and we are bitter or continually angry about something, the Spirit of God can transition us to patience. The qualities that we are transitioned to are the fruit of the Spirit.

To understand what is meant by the fruit of the Spirit we need to enter into the mindset of the ancient world. For a tree to bear good fruit, it had to be the recipient of a good process of cultivation. The tree would have to have a steady supply of water, a supply of fertilizer, and the close attention of the farmer. Then the tree would give good fruit. Good fruit comes from cultivation.

> *As we cultivate a transparent and trusting relationship with God the Father through our identity with Christ, we will be able to bear good fruit through the work of the Spirit.*

As we cultivate a transparent and trusting relationship with God the Father through our identity with Christ, we will be able to bear good fruit through the work of the Spirit. In effect, the good soil is our identity in Christ, the tree trunk and branches are our relationship with God the Father, and the fruit is the work of the Spirit in our lives.

❧ ❧ ❧

Heading into God's Presence

Two friends and I, when we were about 23 or 24, went to Ocean Beach in San Francisco. Near the Golden Gate Bridge, it is a famous place for people to walk the beach and enjoy the view. After we started a fire on the beach, I started walking out into the surf. As the water came above my knees, I felt something odd. The sand was sliding out from under my feet. I stepped forward, and the odd sensation returned. It felt like the sand was being vacuumed out from under my feet. I had never felt anything like that in my life. *Undertow!* was the thought that rushed into my mind. I not only felt the sand being washed out, I also felt I was being pulled toward the ocean.

Whatever you do next better be smart, I thought to myself. Quickly I glanced over my shoulder through the fog to our fire on the beach. *Take one step backward,* I thought, *and then another one—and make sure you go directly backward.*

Looking over my shoulder straight at the fire, I started walking backward. I could tell I was making headway. The waves were now below my knees. Then the water was below my ankles. Finally I was on the dry sand. While I was walking up the beach, my legs were still wet and cold, but I continued to go the direction of the fire. I got there and told my friends what I'd experienced. As we talked, I dried out and became warm and comfortable. Then we resumed enjoying our time.

Sin inside us and the flesh want to create an undertow in our lives that will sweep us toward death. As we sense that powerful undertow and are confused by the fog and the waves, we must fix our eyes on the fire of God the Father's presence and head in His direction. As we do, we will still feel the coldness of the water, the pulling of the undertow, and the sand disappearing under our feet. But we must focus on the Father and head into His presence. When we arrive, we will still be cold and damp, but as we warm ourselves around the Father the effects of the undertow will disappear.

As we live a healthy spiritual life, we will share our lives with God the Father through our acceptance in Christ and be empowered by the Spirit of God. We will constantly be aware of each Person. Each Person of our Triune God has given Himself to the work of helping and encouraging us with our emotions. As we live in the love of the Trinity, we will experience and model God's rich relational life within our own heart.

11

Becoming Who God Intended

$\mathcal{R}$ $\mathcal{R}$ $\mathcal{R}$

W HEN I FIRST BECAME A CHRISTIAN and thought of how the church functioned in the world, there were two comic images I would picture to myself. The first was that of the Three Stooges. I thought of the church that way because the three stooges would bicker and insult each other, and hardly do anything right. When they did do something right, it was quite by accident, and the people watching would laugh at them. The church seemed like a bunch of ineffective and comical buffoons.

The second image was that of Mr. Magoo. Mr. Magoo was a terribly nearsighted man who would miss catastrophe by a hair-breadth. An almost divine set of coincidences would keep him alive and safe. For example, unbeknownst to himself he would walk through a construction project, and as he did so he would avoid accident after accident. He also would rescue the woman in distress or defeat the villains, but he would ever hardly know what was going on.

Of the two images I had, it was probably Mr. Magoo who would be the closest to the biblical picture, because divine providence was always on his side. Yet neither of my pictures was biblical. God has a deeply different perspective on us.

Participating in the Family Business

Why on earth should God the Father—who does indeed have a great deal of intelligence—want a bunch of clowns like us involved in His business? When I became a Christian, I knew very well I had problems, and the longer I was a Christian the more problems I found. (Being from Family Group Three, of course I didn't tell anyone about what I was thinking. I just tried to deal with it on my own.)

Yet the question is very important. It deals with what do we do after we meet the challenge of our own insides. Life has more to it than just being happy and managing our appetites. Everything in the Christian life *starts* with our managing ourselves through the work of the Spirit of God, but it does go on from that. The Christian life goes on from *management of the inner life* to *making a difference in life*.

In a very real sense the least important task, that of managing our own insides, oftentimes takes on the greatest personal significance because of the pain and frustration involved. But God's intention is that after we have managed our own insides, we should go on to the truly greater task of making a difference in the lives around us.

I was meeting with a couple who wanted to marry. But the man was struggling with sexual addiction, and the couple felt that he really should come to terms with the addictive behavior, deal with it, and go on to health. The future wife was defining him almost completely by what he was struggling with. She said, "I can't stand that he's getting sexually excited about some other woman than me. And it's not even a woman; it's just a picture."

With that pressure on him and out of his own sense of failure, he would say, "All I am is a sex addict, and that's all I am."

As we chatted, I remarked that the real tragedy of all this was that the person struggling with addiction reduces himself to not much more than the addiction itself. Way down deep, the addicted know they are more than their addiction, yet nearly every waking moment that is how they define themselves. It is similar to the strategy of the young woman who defines herself by just her weight and appearance.

We are more than what we struggle with, and throughout this book we have talked about how we should look at ourselves in a different way. Having a different picture of ourselves will lead us to new happiness and self-control. But once we have that new picture and a new sense of self-control, our real life of significance begins. That is where we become full partners in the family business.

The way we make a difference in life is to invest ourselves in the family business. God the Father wants us to participate in it. The family atmosphere is love, joy, and peace. The family business is loving and rescuing others. The business is other-centered. The end of life is not having a happy heart; the end of life is having a heavenly heart. A heavenly heart is other-centered because God is love for others.

Our Model: The Other-Centered Life of the Son

Since God the Father is other-centered, He has sent His Son on a mission. This mission has a number of stages to it, but the final goal of this mission is for the Son to reign on the earth. In the Old Testament the mission is described in detail, but again it always ends with the Son reigning over the earth.

> A *child* will be born to us, a *son* will be given to us; and the
> government will rest on His shoulders; and His name will
> be called a Startling Wonder, Counselor, a Warrior God,
> Father of the Endless Future, Prince of Shalom.
>
> There will be no end to the increase of (His) govern-
> ment or of peace on the throne of David and over his
> kingdom, to establish it and to uphold it with equity and
> righteousness *from then on and forevermore*. The zeal of
> Yahweh of armies will accomplish this (Isaiah 9:6-7).

The Son has been given for a great mission, which involves being
sent, serving, suffering, being rewarded, and reigning.

Many Christians indeed know the Son was sent, but they also
need to know about the other stages of the journey. The Son also
served. Jesus was sent on a mission involving pain. The mission
was challenging not only in the great goals that would be achieved
but also in that it involved a great price to be paid. This mission
was one of suffering service. Mark 10:45 says,

> The Son of Man did not come to be served, but to serve,
> and to give His soul (His life) a ransom in place of the many.

Christ invited suffering into His own soul so He could
present that suffering as a satisfaction to God. In this satisfaction God not only has a payment for sin, but the payment
has brought Him to a state of positive pleasure over what the
Son has done with sin. In the context of Isaiah 53 and
Romans 5, the suffering is for those who are rescued by His
blood, and who accept His friendship. His service for God the
Father led directly to the cross. As the baby Jesus lay in the
manger, the shadow of the cross was already falling across
Him. From His home in heaven, He came to the earth to
embrace the cross.

He emptied Himself while taking on the external display of a slave, being in the likeness of men; and as far as external characteristics are concerned being found as a man, He humbled Himself, becoming obedient unto death, the death of the cross (Philippians 2:7).

In heaven the Son was glorious; He was in the external display of deity. But in His heart, He looked at you and said, "This glory is not as important to Me as you are." Then He stepped out of heaven onto the earth to take on the form of a slave. He embraced becoming human as matter-of-factly as we turn off a light switch when we go from one room to another. Coming to earth, He lived out the life of a man. Then He became obedient to death on a cross. (Always remember His love for you. *You* are more important to Him than the pain.)

His Reward and Reign

As a result, the Son was rewarded. Out of profound appreciation for His noble Son, the Father has made Him the center of everything:

Wherefore also God highly exalted and freely gave to Him the Name or reputation that is above every reputation (Philippians 2:9).

Since Jesus freely set aside His majesty to die on the cross, God the Father gave Him the greatest reputation in the universe. No one has ever done or will ever do, or will ever need to do, the same as Jesus.

Since the Son has acted so nobly, the Father wants the teeming life of the universe to acknowledge who the Son is and what He has done. Philippians 2:10 reveals to us the Father's intention:

> In relationship to the Name of Jesus, every knee shall bow in the upper heavens, upon earth, and under the earth.

Sooner or later, those in hell, those on the earth, and those who fill the heavens will have to kneel before Christ, acknowledging who He is and the beauty of what He has done. Every non-Christian will have to acknowledge what he or she was worth to God before being sent into outer darkness.

A New Assignment for Us

Now the Son reigns. As the Great Commission states, all authority in the heavens and on earth has been given to Him. He is now the Head of everything, and He is the Head of the church, His body. After His resurrection He was given the rule of the universe, and as the Head of the body, He commissioned His disciples to change history:

> While continually seeing Him, they worshiped with delighted joy; but some kept jumping between two opinions. And Jesus came to them and spoke to them, saying, "All authority has been given to Me in heaven and on earth. Go therefore and make disciples of all the non-Jews, while baptizing them in the authority and reputation of the Father and the Son and the Holy Spirit" (Matthew 28:17-19).

The disciples were stunned by the experience of Christ's resurrection. Being utterly delighted, they swung back and forth between a state of delirious joy and a state of profound shock. Shock, because all of their life experience told them dead people don't live again. The language that is used literally means to be standing in two different worlds: one world where a man does not rise from the dead, and one world where a man does.

The disciples were in a unique situation. Normally when a person dies, it is an ongoing shock to the loved ones that the deceased has left their lives and will not return. The opposite was true here. The continual shock was having the dead person alive. Jesus dealt with that by giving His disciples something to do. He told them to go conquer the world in the authority of the Trinity. At that point Jesus joined His newly granted authority to a mission for the disciples, one that made them new participants in the family business. He sent them into the world to be part of the family business.

We Are to Replicate the Life Pattern of Jesus

This is where we come again to the question I mentioned at the beginning of this chapter. Why on earth should God the Father want a bunch of clowns like us involved in His business? In my view of all my problems, I missed a few things in the Father's perspective.

We who have been invited into the circle of love predating time, the circle of the Trinity, are now asked to join in the great Family enterprise.

A number of people I know have businesses, and some are family businesses. Other businesses have friends working together. Two dear friends of mine, Brian and Doug, work together in a medical business, and when I think of them, I do not first think of their business, I think of their friendship. Friends want friends to participate in their business! Friends and loved ones like to be together, and what could be more fun than doing something wonderfully significant together?

Christian service is a great gift of friendship God gives His children. On the one hand, His use of us illustrates His acceptance. Even though we are imperfect people, He wants us to participate in the family business. On the other hand, that He uses us also deeply underscores our unity with His Son: As those joined to Christ, we are also invited to replicate His ministry.

The invitation also reflects the unity of the relationship at the heart of everything. We who have been invited into the circle of love predating time, the circle of the Trinity, are now asked to join in the great Family enterprise. Because the Father loves us deeply, He allows us to participate in the goal of Jesus' ministry, the redemption of mankind. His settled desire is to give us the same great goal He gave to His Son.

Our Invitation into the Family Business

As we have seen in the preceding chapters, when we believed the gospel—that Jesus died for us and rose again—God identified us with Christ regardless of our feelings or knowledge of such a reality. Our identification with His life events, His crucifixion, His death, His resurrection, and His suffering are true from God's side of it, no matter what we feel or think. But one area of identification remains where we have to consciously choose to participate. That area is in the replication, or copying, of Christ's life mission. The Son of God was sent to serve, to suffer, to ascend, and to be rewarded. We have been chosen for the same life mission, but just as it was with Jesus, the choice remains for us to participate or not.

This is like being born into an earthly family. The children are genuine members of the family. They also inherit the family history and relationships. But somewhere along the way they have to decide to become productive family members. We have the same choice in the family of God.

After His resurrection, Christ had to basically chase His disciples around town in order to get to talk to them. They had gone into hiding. When He found them in an upper room, He came into the room and scared them half to death. When they saw Him, they thought He was a ghost. For them it was easier to believe in ghosts than in the resurrection from the dead. He had to ask to eat a fish so they would understand He was not a ghost. (This was almost closer to a Three Stooges routine than a glorious resurrection.)

Even in the face of their rampant fear, lack of understanding, and disbelief, He still passed on to them the same commission He had received, the same privilege He was given to fulfill the grand purposes of God.

> Jesus said to them again, "Peace to all of you. Even as the Father has commissioned Me, also I Myself am commissioning you" (John 20:21).

In this same context, He breathed on them and told them to receive the Holy Spirit. He also shared with them the message of forgiveness of sins for others. His life pattern now belonged to them.

Why do we have this privilege? God counts us as mature sons because we have believed in His Son. We have looked beyond His humanity, we have looked beyond His enslavement, and we have seen the Son of God. Because we have seen the Son clothed in human flesh and crucified on the cross, God has turned to us and said, "The rest of the world is blind to Him. But because you have seen Him, I will allow you to participate in His life and His mission."

Responsibilities and Rewards

Christ's mission came to its completion through His resurrection and ascension into heaven. There He was rewarded by being made the Head of the church and head of the universe. God the Father gave Him the Name, or reputation, above all else. Even as God has rewarded Christ in heaven, He has opened the same opportunity to us. Should He really do this, is the question, since we have so many problems and failings?

In answer, let me give an illustration. One of the values of having children is that they supply pictures that the Spirit of God can use to give insight to our nearsighted (Mr. Magoo–like) eyes. As our daughter, Adrianne, entered her later teenage years, we had our share of conflict. At different times she would explain to me that my advice-giving and control of her life was actually more harmful than helpful. She said that when I looked at her I saw an eight-year-old girl and not the young woman she was becoming, and that I should have more confidence in her.

I replied to her, "Adrianne, when I look at you, I see you simultaneously as a baby in my arms, as a toddler, all the way through every stage up to your teen years."

Adrianne challenged that and said that for both of our sakes, I needed to see her just as a young adult. She repeated several times that if I actually gave her the choice when it came to life decisions, I would probably find she did exactly what I would want her to do.

As I eased up, I found that to be true. The more freedom and responsibility she had, the better she did and the more mature she acted. I realized that the only way my daughter was going to get to adulthood was to have responsible choice. Choice with its up and downs is what creates maturity.

I have also found the same to be true with team members in our organization. We get the best out of people only when we trust them with significant responsibilities. When they do make mistakes, we use that as a stepping-stone to greater effectiveness. We don't use it as a reason to browbeat the person. We can only get the best when we trust other people with meaningful responsibilities.

Everyone who has ended up mature has started out as an immature, impulsive, ineffective person. That is where we started out with the gospel. But God the Father wanted to draw maturity out of us, so He has given us large responsibilities along with great enablement, the enablement of the Spirit of God.

God has not only given us large responsibilities, He has also told us what the stepping-stone to large rewards is. We are challenged to replicate Christ's ministry. If we do, the significance of that decision will carry on into heaven itself. For those who have chosen to suffer along with Him will reign with Him. In 2 Timothy 2:12, Paul reminded his associate Timothy of this:

> If we endure, we shall also reign with Him.

When we trust in Christ, God makes our future secure (2 Timothy 2:13). Our part in the future reign is optional, though. Our place in reigning is dependent upon our choice of serving and suffering for Jesus. Paul took for granted the possibility of reigning with Christ, and he wanted Christians to assume the coming reality of this kingdom. To the Corinthian Christians he wrote,

> I want you to reign as kings so that we might reign with you (1 Corinthians 4:8).

Jesus very straightforwardly gave the same as a promise in Revelation 3:21:

He who is overcoming, I will grant to her or him to sit with
Me on my throne to share My authority, as I also overcame
and sat down with My Father to share His authority.

In the Bible, spiritual responsibility is not given to the clever
and well-informed. Responsibility is given to those who love
Christ and choose to serve, and who love others enough to suffer
for them. Even humanly speaking, we have learned in this world
not to trust the promises of the politicians nor the descriptions of
their credentials and the glowing words in their TV ads. In American
society today, the fireman and the policeman are the most
trusted figures because they chose to face suffering and death
during the World Trade Center attack.

Who can we trust? We can trust those who have served faithfully
and suffered nobly. And we can trust Christ with our interests
because He died for us. As we conclude we can trust Him for
our salvation, we also need to conclude that we have to entrust
ourselves to the same life pattern He followed. It is a life pattern
that starts in this life and stretches out into eternity.

So how can we look at this life as Christians? In a true sense
we are tying up our running shoes for eternity. The real race
begins with being ushered into Christ's presence. The reward is
to share in His reign. Our Christian life is a preparation. Now
we are making the decisions, accepting the roles, and sharing the
suffering that will determine what we will be doing for endless
years of time.

The God of infinite imagination spectacularly filled the earth
and the heavens with wondrous forms of life and beauty. Certainly
He will express more power and thought when He rewards
those who have been faithful to His Son.

THE SPIRITUAL LIFE
OF BLESSEDNESS

I have had hidden struggles in my Christian life and growth—struggles I did not want to mention to anyone. One was that I thought Christianity was stupid because it involved God suffering. Why on earth should the God of heaven choose to suffer? It was ridiculous on the face of it! If God was as wonderful and infinite as we Christians say, it seemed to me that with His brainpower He could have figured out a better way of doing things.

Even though I was thinking this, the Lord was kind enough to give me an answer to my question. As Carol and I were married and had children, I noticed something. I did not mind being inconvenienced for our children or my wife. In fact, I did not mind suffering for them. I simply loved them, and the inconvenience and suffering didn't matter. I noticed that friends do not mind suffering for those they love. Lovers are not afraid of pain and inconvenience for those they love. While I was becoming more aware of this, the insight came as God the Spirit took the picture of what I was experiencing in family life and applied it to divine life.

Simply put, healthy persons do not mind suffering for others! God, being infinite health, is not bothered at all with the thought of suffering for His creation. His fallen creation, of course, preoccupied with itself and its self-created problems, looks at the suffering involved with Christianity—the cross—and finds it lacking sense. A loving parent looking at the same reality finds a deep sensibleness to it. The attitude of the parent is what the Bible calls *blessed*, while the attitude of the self-absorbed adult may merely be happy—or at worst, miserably selfish.

As I pointed out earlier, we have studied much about emotions, but the goal of life is more than just being a smooth manager of what is inside us. We have been called to a nobler role. We have seen that we can participate in the family business. We have been made participants in the mission of God the Father and Christ.

Blessedness Is Not Happiness

Not only have we been placed in the family business, we have likewise been called to a greater emotional state than just being happy. We are called to be *blessed*. Being blessed is something profoundly greater than just being happy. Consider the Beatitudes in Matthew 5. Blessedness is more than happiness; it is deeper than happiness.

> *Blessed* are the *poor* in spirit, for theirs is the kingdom of heaven.
>
> *Blessed* are those who are continually *mourning*, for they shall be comforted.
>
> *Blessed* are those who *hunger* and *thirst* for righteousness, for they shall be satisfied.
>
> *Blessed* are those who have been *persecuted* for the sake of righteousness, for theirs is the kingdom of heaven.
>
> *Blessed* are you when you are *insulted* and *persecuted*, and falsely all kinds of *evil are said against you* because of Me.

Blessing and Pain

Blessedness more often than not has a negative attached to it. In the Beatitudes a person was blessed if he or she continually mourned, was hungry and thirsty, or was being insulted, persecuted, and falsely accused. The common thread is that the blessed person is suffering the ills and insults of life. Seemingly one cannot have such blessing without pain.

This mating of blessing and pain is also common in the rest of the New Testament. Blessedness involves correct suffering. The word "blessed" appears in each of the following contexts with an area of pain.

James said the person was blessed who persevered under trials because, with the Lord's approval, he or she would receive the crown of life. The negative was the trial, and the positive blessing was the crown of life.

> Blessed is a person who perseveres under trial; for once he has been approved, he will receive the crown of life, which has been promised to those who love Him (James 1:12).

In Corinthians 7, Paul the apostle gave advice about divorce and remarriage. He said that a wife was bound to her husband as long as he was alive. But she could remarry if he died. But then he advised the woman that she would be more blessed if she remained unmarried (verse 40). Oftentimes many Christian singles view their singleness as a curse. Yet this is, in fact, the only time in the New Testament that the phrase "more blessed" occurs. All the other times it is just the word *blessed*. The important thing to notice is the negative reality of being single, and the positive reality that God can turn it into a blessing.

The apostle Peter told the believers that if they were threatened and intimidated, they were blessed:

> Even if you should suffer for the sake of righteousness, you are blessed. And do not fear their intimidation, and do not be troubled (1 Peter 3:14).

The context tells us that the blessing was experiencing life as Christ experienced it. Again we have the contrast of the positive and the negative. The great goal in life is not necessarily to experience happiness all the time—the great goal is to experience Christ.

Peter later repeated the theme that the godly Christian would be reviled. If that happened, the Christian was blessed because Peter took for granted that the Spirit of glory and of God would rest on them (1 Peter 4:14). Peter was assuming that the presence of the Spirit was in the believer and that He would cause the life of Christ to be manifested. When that happened, it would lead to persecution and the attaining of the blessing.

The Deep Comfort of God

Though Scripture speaks many times of the blessings that God will pour out upon His own, it singles out how painful experiences will enable a Christian to be blessed. This enables us to find something deeper and more meaningful than just feeling good. The deeper and more meaningful experience is to discover the comfort and fellowship of God; this goes deeper than pain.

> *A Christian's joy should always be deeper than a Christian's pain.*

In fact, the realities of the spiritual life transcend emotion. Blessedness is correctly perceiving suffering and responding to it in an emotionally healthy way. The person who is blessed is peaceful, but often with an area of pain within the heart. The blessed person deals with that in a biblical way without becoming irresponsible or insensible, having discovered that God's comfort can go deeper than pain.

Here is a great principle: *A Christian's joy should always be deeper than a Christian's pain.* Many individuals assume that a person is either happy or sad. For them nothing exists in the middle, nor do emotions such as happiness and sadness operate simultaneously. The Bible assumes that people are more sophisticated than that. In reference to being blessed, two simultaneous emotions go on at the same time: joy and pain. The joy of God's comfort and the pain are present simultaneously.

People are scared to death of suffering. But one of the privileges a Christian has is learning not to be afraid of pain—because God's comfort can go deeper than pain. We can learn from the Lord that emotional states are multifaceted. For instance, in the book of Romans Paul said,

> I am telling the truth in Christ, I am not lying, my conscience continually testifying with me in the Holy Spirit, that I have great sorrow and unceasing grief in my heart (Romans 9:1-2).

He was very sad over the condition of his Jewish relatives. In contrast to that, he also told the recipients of the letter to the Romans that God has every variety of joy available to the Christian through the power of the Holy Spirit (15:13). These statements are not contradictory if we recognize that a person can have different emotional states going on at the same time.

We are complex creatures and our emotional life is complex. Our desires are also multifaceted. Ephesians 2:3 says that various desires exist, the desires of the flesh and the mind. A person can have competing desires and competing emotions present simultaneously. In Philippians, Paul said he had competing desires: One was to stay alive and minister to his fellow Christians, and the other was to be present with God in heaven, which was far better (1:23-24).

A Christian can have an area of pain with a companion comfort. Mere happiness can be understood as undiluted joy based upon everything within and without being good. Blessedness, though, flies in the face of such mere happiness because it finds meaning in our imperfect world. Blessedness means that the person has transcended the circumstance and the stress to find a deeper source of comfort.

Jesus' Blessedness

Christ was blessed. He had a rich emotional life that included suffering, but it was dominated by the emotions of joy, love, and peace. Even when facing the cross, He said to His disciples that He wanted them to share His inner tranquility:

> These things I have spoken to you that My joy may be in you, and your joy may be made full (John 15:11).

He said to His disciples in Matthew,

> Come unto me, all you that are laboring to exhaustion and are completely loaded down, and I will give you rest. Take my yoke upon you, and be discipled by me; for I am easygoing and humble in heart: and you shall find rest unto your souls. For my yoke is kindly, and my burden is light (Matthew 11:29-30).

In the face of religious fanaticism, He could describe Himself as easygoing, a Person without edges. That was the disposition He normally had. In the face of death, He could describe Himself as peaceful.

Though Christ maintained positive emotions, He freely experienced the painful emotions all of us have had to struggle through. His emotional reactions were full and deep. At the tomb of Lazarus, He wept so obviously that the observing Pharisees noted how much He liked his dead friend (John 11:35). And though He wept at the death of Lazarus, He wailed over the unbelief of Jerusalem. In Luke 19:41, as He rode a donkey into Jerusalem, at the brow of the hill where the city came into view, He broke into heaving sobs of grief. Death brought tears to His eyes, but the unbelief of Israel and their refusal to be gathered in by Him reduced Him to heartbroken sobbing. He was not a stranger to the range of uncomfortable emotions from irritation to depression.

In the Garden, the night before His crucifixion, Jesus was anguished, depressed, and despondent (Matthew 26:37). That experience drove Him into the depths of pain and depression. It was not play-acting. Jesus was horrified by what He anticipated, and He asked the Father if there was any possible way for Him to avoid the test. Receiving the answer that none existed, He worked through what from our perspective are incomprehensible emotions so He could bring us to God the Father.

He also experienced the frustrations that life brings. He was angered (Mark 3:5). He was annoyed (Mark 10:14). In a lively and lovingly etched comment, the Greek text says that Jesus showed real irritation with the way His disciples were treating children:

> When Jesus saw this, He snorted with indignation and said to them, "Permit the children to come to Me; stop hindering them; for the kingdom of God belongs to such as these."

At other times He deeply groaned over the unbelief of those around Him (Mark 8:12). The Pharisees had come to Him to ask for a sign from heaven. After all of His miracles, they still wanted proof. He refused to give them proof and at the same time displayed frustration and irritation.

To experience the life of Christ means for us that we experience the full gamut of emotions the way Christ would have experienced them. The spiritual life is not to be a bundle of bliss. The spiritual life is the blessedness of experiencing the ups and downs of life the way Jesus experienced them. That is true blessedness!

The Feast of Comfort Deeper than Pain

Jesus' relationships and values left Him the master of His emotional life. His emotions were morally managed within the greater context of God's will and provisions. As believers, therefore, we have not only the principles and commands of Scripture to help us manage our emotional lives, we also have the example of our Lord Jesus Christ.

For us the end result is that life should be a feast, that all emotions and experiences become part of a richly satisfying banquet. Life has much to offer, both bad and good, but God has the capacity to bring happiness into it, and bring blessing into its difficult parts:

> All the days of the afflicted are bad, but a good heart is a continual feast (Proverbs 15:15).

The truly marvelous part of being made in the image of God and being an emotional creature is that we have the privilege of sensing God's good comfort within. One time during an Easter service, I was seated listening to a reading from the Gospels describing how Christ was misunderstood and frustrated by His disciples. I was not in a particularly good mood because some friends in ministry had treated me in what from my perspective was a shabby way. I was depressed and upset. As I was listening to the Gospel accounts, the Spirit of God said to my heart, "If they did those things to Jesus, what is it that you expect?" Suddenly my mood changed. I realized that the emotional suffering that I was going through was normal—not a surprise—and part of life in Christ. As that dawned on me, a deeper peace than the depth of my frustrations entered my heart. I went from pain to blessedness.

We are called to be more than happy. We are called to be blessed. Being blessed means that the life of Christ is present within our hearts. Being blessed means that we have the life of God in our midst. Being blessed means that we have the wonderful privilege of discovering that God's comfort goes deeper than our pain.

❧ ❧ ❧

Getting Ready for the Tomorrows

The great goal of the spiritual life is not to become a puddle of bliss. It is, rather,

- 🍃 to have an emotional life like Jesus Christ's emotional life
- 🍃 to have a ministry like Jesus Christ's ministry
- 🍃 and to have the same blessedness that Jesus Christ did

God has not only shared with us a union with Christ, He also is sharing with us a quality of life and ministry like Christ's. As the Son was sent to serve, suffer, ascend, be rewarded, and reign, we are sent as sons and daughters to serve, suffer, ascend, be rewarded, and to reign. As we suffer, we also will have the privilege of being blessed.

The goal is that the picture that we are in—that of being joined to Christ—may become an emotional and relational reality. As Paul has said, to live is Christ!

You and I value being happy. But happiness is nothing compared to what God can do in our lives today—and what He intends to do for us throughout eternity. Today is just the time for us to lace up our running shoes for eternity. Today is the time to experience blessedness. Today is the time to experience the life of Christ in the here and now.

But endless tomorrows will come. With those tomorrows will come the joining of how God sees us now with the life of the future. God's perception and our reality will finally become one!

Questions for Small Groups

INTRODUCTION

The heart of Christianity is relationships. Christianity has at its center one God who coexists in the wondrous love and communion of the Trinity. Relationship then, is the core of reality. At the heart of everything is never ending goodness, pure and happy relationship.

Christianity is knowing God through Jesus Christ. It is simply having a relationship with God. The benefits are many. Initially we are reparented by God and afterwards we have the privilege of growing in a loving friendship.

The book Becoming Who God Intended is designed to help our relationships with one

another and with God. This book presents God's treatment of His children as the model for healthy relationships. As we grow in our knowledge of God, the natural overflow should be improved relationships with others.

ABOUT THE BOOK

Dr. David Eckman enjoys people and has a heart for the person in pain. He is convinced that understanding God's ways is pivotal for the healthy, emotional life of the Christian and non-Christian. Dr. Eckman has spent over 25 years in biblical research and has spent over 20 years developing the material for the transformational studies of which Becoming Who God Intended is a part.

Is the resource book for both singles and married people?

Yes! Regardless of your marital status, healthy emotions are necessary in all facets of life. Because this material focuses on emotions in general, it is equally beneficial for both Christians and non-Christians. Everyone needs to learn how to understand and manage their emotions, and this book gives you the necessary resources.

How is the book structured?

In Becoming Who God Intended, Dr. Eckman not only presents Biblical principles regarding our emotions, but he also focuses on applications that we can make to our everyday life. These applications are also unique because they involve our imagination and the pictures that are instinctive within us. Also the Bible translations in the book are his own.

Should my small group read through each chapter together?

No. Each person should be reading the book on his/her own and reflect on the contents. Group discussion is enhanced when each person has read the material and comes prepared to share.

Part 1:
Did God Make a Mistake When He Gave Us Emotions?

Chapter 1: Sure I'm a Christian, But --

Chapter Summary:

Day to day, many Christians live alienated from God. Sure, we go to church and go through the motions. Yes, we're going to heaven—yes, the Bible is full of good principles to live by. But where we really live, feel, and think...in our heart of hearts... God seems irrelevant. The Bible doesn't touch us there. We are disappointed in Christianity, and feel disconnected from God and from others.

We suffer from fear, anger, and depression—and are often trapped in thinking and behavior that we hate. We feel guilty and ashamed over the way we are. We're afraid to even ask the question, "does God even care?" Then we perform to get acceptance. But though we keep trying harder, we end up more alienated.

The author experienced all this. He grew up in an alcoholic family, and though he came to know Jesus in high school, his emotions remained frozen. But God started a change by breaking through to him with a stunning picture of His love.

Unless we place ourselves in the pictures of God's truth— using the power of healthy imagination—biblical truth will not touch our emotions, and we will not truly understand it. True biblical spirituality is the best way to be emotionally healthy.

1. Do you think that many in churches are living disconnected lives, their emotional life does not match at all what they profess to believe? Is this a problem? Why?

2. Agape is the Greek word from the New Testament that is used of God's love. It means that God has a passionate delight in persons. It's more than just an act of the will, as is often taught. If more people believed that, how would that affect how they feel about God and themselves?

3. What are your observations on the comment that many churches move new believers along too fast? Instead the new believer needs to be slowed down and nurtured in their new life in Christ.

Chapter 2: Trapped in the Mood Cycle

Chapter Summary:

The mood cycle is composed of three parts: a negative or painful mood within, a desire for something to kill the pain within, and wrongful activity that hurts oneself and often others. That cycle is directly challenged in the New Testament of the Bible. The mood cycle also is at the heart of addiction. Sadly guilt and shame and unhealthy religion can make the mood cycle and addiction far worse!

Negative emotions include worry, anxiety, fear, low-level discontent and depression. They don't exist just by themselves. They feed into an addictive cycle that traps us in controlling sinful desires, habits, and addictions. Paul the apostle gives the bigger picture of the mood cycle, which for so many Christians becomes like a hangman's noose. As we live in this way, we become further bound by guilt and shame. We exist in a state of doubt— "continually reexamining," according to Scripture. And this is the condition in which so many believers today find themselves.

1. What are your thoughts on "what we do with our emotions will almost predetermine what we do with our will and relationships (page 29, and see chart on page 21)"?

2. What do you think about the idea that the real problem in addiction is unaddressed pain?

3. What part does emotional eating play for many in their inability not to lose weight?

4. Have one of the members read Ephesians 2:4-5 from the bottom of page 52 of the book. Does God emotionally delight in us or did He have to make us lovable, first? What do you think about that? How does that make you feel?

Chapter 3: Are Emotions Christian?

Chapter Summary:

Emotional health is a major cultural issue—both in American culture and church culture. There is a deep hunger among evangelicals to have their emotions touched and involved in their faith, and to feel God's love and desire for them and enjoyment of them. We must acknowledge the place of emotions because they define our inner world. We misrepresent and misunderstand God and His Word if we "weed out" emotions.

1. What do you think of the author's idea that "**emotions do not authenticate truth, but emotions do authenticate our understanding and integration of the truth?**" Can you think of examples of what it looks like when emotions and truths line up? Can you think of examples of what it looks like when emotions and truths do not line up?

2. How can we line up more of what we feel with what we know? How we help each other and our families to do the same?

3. Have you had the experience of being around a person or a religious organization that motivates people to action by guilt, shame or worthlessness? What is the fallout of this? Now, have you ever been motivated to do something because of a passionate enjoyment of another person (for example, you were madly in love with someone)? How does the motivation make a difference?

Chapter 4: You Can't Live Without Them

Chapter Summary:

In Chapter 4 we find that God is deeply emotional. As a reflection of the divine, everything about us is an insight into deity, including our emotions! As an important step toward emotional health, we need to realize that our emotions matter to God and to us. A true spiritual life is a life overflowing with healthy emotions such as love, joy, and peace; a carnal or unspiritual lifestyle is one based in emotional pain and turmoil.

1. In the original biblical languages, "spirit" implies self-awareness, reflection, and will. "Soul" implies sensation, feelings, and appetites. God is spirit and has a soul. People have flesh, souls, and spirits. What does this say about God and man?

2. A healthy spiritual relationship with God generates what kind of powerful emotions? Describe what it is like to experience or observe these emotions in ourselves or others.

3. What do you think about the idea that the essence of an unspiritual life is emotional pain and turmoil (page 80)?

Part 2:
The Power of a Picture

Chapter 5: The Imagination is the Key

Chapter Summary:

Isn't the imagination dangerous? What about its potential for evil? What about "graven images"? The truth is, Jesus came to redeem our emotional life. He shows this in the Sermon on the Mount, in which he talks about the imagination and the emotions.

The role of the imagination is crucial in reforming our emotions and our view of who we are—and in giving us "radical permission" to have a transparent relationship with God. This gives us the basis for controlling our moods and desires—that is, managing our emotions. If we allow God to place healthy, biblical pictures within our minds, this leads to, in turn, healthy perspectives, healthy relationships, and healthy emotions.

1. What are your thoughts on the proper use of the imagination and do you think that such proper use will deeply and positively change our lives?

2. Why do you think that for some religious people doing things a certain way seems to be more important than people or the existence of God Himself?

3. What are your thoughts on the following Bible verses?

   "Blessed are the ones who have no more energy, have given up on their own efforts, who are poor in spirit, for theirs is the kingdom of God.

   Blessed are the ones who are continually mourning, for they shall be comforted."

   Matthew 5:3-4

4. Why is our will unable to dismiss depression, bid guilt be gone, and tell despair to disappear?

5. If it is true that God the Father takes care of us whether we trust Him or not, how should that affect how we view life and experience our emotions?

6. What are your thoughts on: "God is a good-hearted Dad who gets a charge out of giving good things to His children" (page 107)?

Chapter 6: New Pictures for Old Ones

Chapter Summary:

Here are examples of healthy pictures from the Bible and from life—and how they can affect and then transform our lives. God puts these kinds of pictures into our hearts and minds more often than we might think, but we often ignore them. However, they can help us tremendously to respond to God as our true, ultimate Father—which is the basis for maturing in the Christian life.

1. What words would you use to describe your "family picture album"?

2. Please take the family background quiz on pages 249-250. Then ask those present to physically divide up into three groups depending upon their scores.

   • Ask members of each group: How did the father in the home function?

   • Ask members of each group: Do you think the way he functioned has influenced your perspective and picture of God as a Father?

   • Ask members of each group: Do you feel that God loves you and likes you?

   • Ask members of each group: Do you have problems trusting people?

   • Ask members of each group: Did you have to earn affection and love in your growing up years?

Chapter 7: God the Father's Favorite Pictures

Chapter Summary:

God the Father has a favorite set of pictures that He is determined to share with us. Those pictures involve what Jesus Christ has done on our behalf. He has suffered, died, been raised from the dead, and has ascended to the Father's throne in Heaven. God has joined us to those pictures so that when He looks at His Son He sees us, and when He looks at us He sees His Son. On top of that, He sees us participating in those central events of Christ's life.

1. What is the favorite picture that you have in your apartment or home?

2. What are your feelings about the central events of Christ's life being counted to be also the central events of your own?

3. How does it feel to have the same quality of relationship with God that Jesus has?

4. What are your thoughts on the statement: "We are not the sum total of our failures but we are the sum total of what Christ has done for us"?

Part 3:
Grasping the Love of the Father, the Son, and the Holy Spirit

Chapter 8: You're a Grown-Up Now

Chapter Summary:

We need to grasp and picture to ourselves that we've been transferred from our earthly family into a new family. This is the bedrock foundation for dealing with moods and replacing them with the fruit of the Spirit. But in this new family, we're not just dependent kids. No—we've finally come into our own (been "adopted," according to the apostle Paul— given the full rights and responsibilities of mature sons). Our "heavenly Dad" has entrusted us with His full resources. Because He has trusted us and fully accepts us, we can now live a life based on trusting Him.

1. What are the three most emotionally significant events in your life?

2. Why is it so important to God the Father that Christians should realize He wants them to function as principled, affectionate adults?

3. What hinders people from entering into the circle of love that God is trying to create for us?

4. When a person feels securely loved, what does that do for their relationships?

5. How do you feel that God has entrusted the Son's great mission to us?

Chapter 9: God's Love – It's Not What You Think It Is

Chapter Summary:

Agape—does it mean that the Father just holds His nose and wills Himself to love us? No! The church has profoundly misunderstood what divine love is. God completely accepts us and passionately delights in us, as illustrated in the Song of Songs and other places in Scripture. In fact, all three members of the Godhead demonstrate their passion for us. God loves you so much that you were worth a Son to Him. And now, unbelievably, we too can love as He does—with agape love.

1. Do you believe for many persons they believe that God loves them because that is His "job"?

2. Based on your observations of the churches that you have been around: What is the percentage of people within those churches who have a deep sense of being loved by God?

3. What are your thoughts about God's love being intense, personal, passionate, and sacrificial?

4. How would people's lives be affected if they thought that God has an intense, personal liking for them?

5. Why do you think the "religious types" were upset with Jesus over His liking tax collectors and non-law-practicing Jews?

6. What are your thoughts about the fact that the God of Heaven gets happy when we open our hearts to a relationship with Him?

Chapter 10: The Model for Life

Chapter Summary:

We share the same relationship with the Father that Jesus has. We are as free to relate to Him as His Son is. Furthermore, we have the very person of our loving God within us through the presence of the Holy Spirit. As we walk according to the Spirit, we can continually defeat the mood cycle and step further into the experience of the life of the triune God.

1. Why is avoiding an area of moral struggle almost guaranteeing defeat in that area?

2. What are your thoughts on the observation that powerful desires often arise out of painful emotional states?

3. Can you give an example of a picture from the past that has had a profound influence on your life?

4. Is it true that many people are afraid of trusting the Gospel (Jesus died for us so that through faith we can have a relationship with God the Father) because they are afraid God will take away good things out of their life, and just give them painful things?

5. A major part of maturity is learning how to transition from painful emotions to positive ones. What are examples in your life of transitioning from painful emotions to positive ones?

Chapter 10: Becoming Who God Intended

Chapter Summary:

God didn't create us just to experience the happiness that comes from properly managing our emotions. In His overwhelming love, He has a far greater purpose for us—to live out blessedness. As we live according to His design, we will experience a life that matches our long-held expectations of what Christianity promises.

1. What is your reaction to Christ's attitude that you are more important to Him than the comforts and glory of Heaven?

2. What is your reaction to the thought that God the Father's goal for you is to follow the life pattern of Jesus Christ?

3. How is it true that maturity results from freedom and choice?

4. What are your thoughts about: "Blessedness is correctly perceiving suffering and responding to it in an emotionally healthy way (page 242)"?

5. What do you think of Jesus "as a person without edges (page 244)"?

6. Have you had experiences of God's comfort going deeper than pain?

Appendix
Family Background Questionnaire

Circle "Yes" or "No" in answer to the following questions as they relate to your family of origin.

Y N Did you ever feel tension dealing with family members?

Y N Did you feel you had to be extremely careful in how you responded to family members?

Y N Did some family members behave as if they were driven by inner tensions, urges, or desires?

Y N Did people in your family act the way they did because they felt they had to maintain an image (not because they felt free to be themselves)?

Y N Were any family members constantly critical of other family members?

Y N Did you feel more accepted by family members when you were doing well than when you were not?

Y N Did family members verbally attack each other when there was a conflict?

Y N Was it sometimes hard to know what a family member was thinking or feeling by what he or she said?

Y N   Was there a dominant person in your family that others
       worked around?

Y N   Did you feel the need to go along with certain family
       members to keep the peace?

Y N   Did you feel uncomfortable to be yourself with your family
       members?

Y N   Did you feel uncomfortable to say what you felt or thought
       around family members?

Y N   Was your home a place you would *not* have chosen to go
       when you wanted to relax or have fun?

Y N   Did you sometimes get tense with the prospect of a family
       gathering?

Y N   Do you consider the atmosphere in the family you were
       brought up in to be more or less normal?

*Count the number of questions to which you answered "Yes." You can
ask the same questions for your present family and again tally the
number of questions to which you reply "Yes."*

   Scoring*: 1–5 = healthy; 6–10 = confused; 11–15 = stressed, or
dysfunctional.*

A Healthy Family

A healthy family has a clear, positive identity, deep affection, and happiness skills. The parents have come to a healthy resolution concerning their family background.

A Confused Family

A confused family has evident affection, limited happiness skills, and unclear identities. The parents have not come to a healthy resolution concerning their family background.

A Dysfunctional Family

A dysfunctional family is unhappy, has long-term stress due to alcoholism or drugs or other addictive behaviors, suffers from cultural collapse, and often has physical or emotional abuse or neglect in the home. The identities are non-existent at best or negative at worst.

BECOMING WHAT GOD INTENDED SEMINARS
An Invitation to Experience God's Loyal Love

BWGI Seminars is a nonprofit ministry dedicated to proclaiming God the Father's loyal love, the efficacy of Christ's work, and the power of the believer's identification with Him.

We offer the following resources:

- ❦ worldwide Christian leadership training

- ❦ seminars

- ❦ community outreaches

- ❦ small-group resources

- ❦ our new e-learning courses

A Personal Invitation

David Eckman invites you to contact BWGI Seminars for a free small-group study guide to use with this book. It contains an introductory session plus 11 study and discussion portions so your group can study and reflect on each of the chapters in this book. Send your request to **orders@bwgi.org**.

David also invites you to join him online for a sample session on worth and identity based on a careful look at Romans chapters 5 and 6. *This is free for you.* Through video, audio, Powerpoint, and creative and accurate translations of the Bible, let him show you the wonderful truths about your worth and identity—truths that are actually in the Bible! Go to **www.bwgi.org/more** for this session.

How to Contact BWGI Seminars

Web site: www.WhatGodIntended.com
Address: BWGI Seminars
             PO Box 5246
             Pleasanton, CA 94566
Telephone: **(925) 846-6264**
E-mail: orders@bwgi.org

Seminars

BWGI Seminars offers a total of 5 seminars. Each one has a lasting impact on individuals and transforms their relationship with God.

We have a team of talented and experienced presenters that will make any seminar an event to remember. Please visit our Web site at www.BWGI.org or call us at 925-846-6264 for more information on seminar bookings for your church or organization.

❦ Setting the Heart Free

This seminar focuses on freeing the heart from guilt and worthlessness so a believer can experience an adult relationship with God, which is not based on performance. This results in an ability to live the Christian life with lasting gratitude.

❦ Healthy Relationships

Healthy relationships flow out of healthy identities, compassionate listening, and other-centeredness. The seminar teaches attendees how to acquire such abilities, and what it means to be made in the image of God. It goes on to address what it means to be male and female.

❦ Addiction Proofing Your Life and Family

Discover how a healthy spirituality directly challenges addiction. This seminar addresses four of the most common addictions that cause individuals and ministries to fall: food, sex, alcohol, and gambling. Identifying gender differences in regards to addictions, it equips participants with biblical principles that have proven effective for breaking addiction.

❦ Healthy Leadership

This seminar presents biblically based principles of leadership for the leader, the team, and the congregation. Everything flows out of our identity with Christ. It goes beyond sterile principles to show how the leader can influence others through relationships, goal-setting, and creating a healthy leadership environment.

❦ Creating a Healthy Family

This seminar is an excellent outreach event, partnering BWGI Seminars and sponsoring churches within a community. The event consists of a three-hour community lecture on family relationships, followed by seven weeks of small-group meetings. The small groups are formed from interested participants after the lecture. (Typically, more than a third of those who attend the lecture choose to join a small group.)

Products and Resources

BWGI Seminars produces books, audiotape sets, pamphlets, and video materials designed to help you grow and mature spiritually in Christ. Our materials have been proven over many years, and we are confident about their effectiveness in restoring the dynamic personal relationship with Christ that God the Father intends for all believers.

Books by David Eckman

❧ Becoming What God Intended: A Study for Spiritual Transformation
This life-changing 186-page workbook is designed to help the Christian achieve an emotionally rich spiritual life in the presence of God. **Price: $20.00**

❧ Knowing the Heart of the Father
Discover the Four truths that will change your life. iscover what often stands in the way of them and how you can begin to know the heart of the Father in a deeper way as He works with these realities into your life. **Price: $15.00**

❧ Creating a Healthy Family: Breaking the Dysfunctional Cycle
This 165-page, 6-week workbook, the first in a series, gives a strategy for both short-term and long-term change. It explains the effects of a stressful family background on an adult, and how that can be positively changed. **Price: $18.00**

❧ Healthy Relationships for Singles & Couples
This book is designed to naturally follow *Creating a Healthy Family*. It addresses how individuals should function in relationships. The goal of this book is to teach how to become an interdependent team. **Price: $18.00**

Audiotapes and CDs by David Eckman

❧ Becoming What God Intended: A Study for Spiritual Transformation
This series of 12 talks forms the background for the *Becoming What God Intended* workbook, acting as a Christian life conference for those who are ready for God to be the change agent for their inner lives. **Price: $40.00**

❧ Setting the Heart Free
This set of six talks is a study in the book of Romans that isolates the three core values that change human personality: a guilt-free environment, a

worthwhile relationship with God as Father, and a new identity in Christ. Price: $22.00

❧ From Tears to Diamonds
This series of four talks describes how a person can deal with the great tragedies of life, explaining not only how to understand such tragedies, but also how to find benefit from them. **Price: $25.00**

❧ Life After Death: Learn How to Rid Your Heart of the Fear of Death
Gain the confidence every person needs when thinking about death. The victory of Christ is not just over sin, the devil, the world, and guilt—it is also a victory over death. In this talk, Dr. Eckman looks at several passages of Scripture to see how Christ has conquered death and how we have victory over death through Him. God's intention is that the great enemy of humanity, death, should not blackmail you! **Price: $7.00**

❧ Knowing God's Heart: Learn How God Views You—It's Better Than You Think!
All of us carry around a picture of ourselves painted across our hearts that is the foundation for all of our relationships. God's picture of the Christian is deeply connected to His Son. Through faith, we have been joined to Christ, and that union is the basis of a truly healthy relationship with God. **Price: $7.00**

❧ Identity in Christ: Learn How to Rid Your Heart of Guilt and Shame
The discovery that God is not preoccupied with your sin sets the stage for realizing the power of the love of God to be experienced and expressed in your life. Discover how the ancient descriptions of the tabernacle in Exodus and Leviticus reinforce the truth of where God's heart is. As you listen, allow these truths of the gospel of Jesus Christ to wash over you and transform your relationship to Jesus to one of deep appreciation, acceptance, and love. **Price: $7.00**

DVD by David Eckman

❧ Creating a Healthy Family: Breaking the Dysfunctional Cycle
This four-part video lecture (two videotapes) gives a strategy for both short-term and long-term change, explaining the effects of a stressful family background on an adult, and how that can be positively changed. The video addresses the emotional scars underlying compulsive behavior, confusion, and diminished self-worth, offering solutions that

are immediately applicable. The tapes are broken into four sections to facilitate use with small groups. Use the workbook in conjunction with this video series for best impact. **Price: $33.00**

E-Learning

Based on the seminars and courses taught for many years, BWGI Seminars will be offering unique e-learning ("distance learning") courses from our Web site, **www.BWGI.org**. A number of different levels will be available, depending on your situation, budget, and available time. The courses will also be available for credit from several institutions of higher learning.

BWGI Seminars' e-learning courses begin with the materials similar to a typical distance-learning course. But that is where the similarities end. BWGI Seminars' courses include access to and interaction with a course mentor. The course mentor is very familiar with the course material—typically having taught it or assisted with the teaching process at seminars and in classrooms. The student communicates with the mentor in several ways: via an online password-protected forum, a private messenger system, and by telephone.

The mentor is available for answering questions and giving assistance in areas of confusion and difficulty. In addition, the mentor will ask questions of the student to gauge progress and understanding level. Quizzes and papers will be expected from the student, and feedback from the mentor will be provided on submitted homework. In the case of a student seeking course credit, a grade will be assigned at the end of the course.

The first course being offered is—

❧ *Spiritual Life Development*
2 semester hours work
This profoundly biblical course is designed to integrate the core values of Christianity into a person's instincts as well as create an emotionally rich environment within, resulting in a truly outward-focused person. This will occur within lectures that are richly Bible-based. It can be taken for credit or noncredit on the graduate level.